Advancing Towards
An Understanding

Robert L. K. Mazibuko

cover designed by
Luthando Mazibuko(M.F.A.)
Edited by Peter Persicaner

BALBOA.
PRESS
A DIVISION OF HAY HOUSE

Balboa Press books may be ordered through booksellers or by contacting:

Balboa Press
A Division of Hay House
1663 Liberty Drive
Bloomington, IN 47403
www.balboapress.com
1 (877) 407-4847

Because of the dynamic nature of the Internet, any web addresses or
links contained in this book may have changed since publication and
may no longer be valid. The views expressed in this work are solely those
of the author and do not necessarily reflect the views of the publisher,
and the publisher hereby disclaims any responsibility for them.

The author of this book does not dispense medical advice or prescribe the use
of any technique as a form of treatment for physical, emotional, or medical
problems without the advice of a physician, either directly or indirectly. The
intent of the author is only to offer information of a general nature to help
you in your quest for emotional and spiritual well-being. In the event you use
any of the information in this book for yourself, which is your constitutional
right, the author and the publisher assume no responsibility for your actions.

Any people depicted in stock imagery provided by Getty Images are
models, and such images are being used for illustrative purposes only.
Certain stock imagery © Getty Images.

Print information available on the last page.

ISBN: 978-1-9822-0356-6 (sc)
ISBN: 978-1-9822-0357-3 (e)

Balboa Press rev. date: 05/02/2018

Contents

Foreword

This booklet was written at the request of Lee Olson who with Ann Arp and Milton Bullock were so encouraging in the early days of my arrival in the United States and acted as a guide at the House of Worship in Wilmette, Illinois. While I hope I have accurately presented the Bahá'í Faith, what follows consists of my own thoughts and views, based on the knowledge that Bahá'ís are charged by the Author of their faith to independently search for truth at all times and in all issues…. this attitude being the first law of their faith as stated by the Center of their Covenant in a well known recorded text.. Following is one example where this law is mentioned.

> **There have issued, from His mighty Pen, various teachings for the prevention of war, and these have been scattered far and wide.**
>
> **The first is the independent investigation of truth; for blind imitation of the past will stunt the mind. But once every soul inquireth into truth, society**

will be freed from the darkness of continually repeating the past.

Selections from the Writings of
Abdu'l-Baha, p. 248

A word of gratitude is expressed for the invaluable assistance of Dale and Kathleen Lehman, who caused this booklet to be altered from its original form to the present. The author is very appreciative of their assistance, as well as that provided by all those persons in, whose names are mentioned herein with whose association the author found enrichment..

Preface

The *Kitáb-i-Iqán—The Book of Certitude*—is a difficult book to understand, perhaps because the Author of the Bahá'í Revelation has meant His religion to last at least a thousand or thousands of years in a religious cycle that spans hundreds of millennia. Yet Bahá'u'lláh's Revelation is for the here and now as well as for the distant future and holds particular urgency for the present generation. Apprehending some measure of its vast treasures can only be done through prayer, good deeds, and repeated study of the Book. Without these, the Book remains locked.

My journey into the *Kitáb-i-Íqán* began by being thrown headlong into it: I was asked to translate it into Xhosa, my native African tongue. The challenge proved immense. I had to distance myself from African ideologies and cultural expectations so as to translate the words as they stand. In the process, the Bahá'í teaching that we are children of one God who loves and cares for all, helped me to maintain focus: I have long held that I am a Bahá'í first, an African second, as all Bahá'ís of all races of origin work for the intended aim of uniting humankind into one large family; along the way, I would discover answers to many of my own spiritual and religious questions, and begin the lifelong process of advancing towards better understanding.

Before going further I must state clearly that what follows is not an interpretation of the *Kitáb-i-Íqán* but merely a collection of personal reflections on its contents and related materials from other Holy Books. I undertook this at the request of some Bahá'í friends, and did so with considerable trepidation lest mere personal opinion be confused with something more significant. However, every Bahá'í is by belief an instructor of the Faith espoused. In the Bahá'í Faith, authoritative interpretation of the Sacred Texts is the sole province of the Center of the Covenant, 'Abdu'l-Bahá, and the Guardian, Shoghi Effendi. Nevertheless, the Universal House of Justice notes that study and development of our personal understandings of the Word of God are crucial aspects of spiritual development, while every Bahá'í is called to teach their Faith to receptive souls after they themselves are convinced of its truths, as taught.

> "A clear distinction is made in our Faith between authoritative interpretation and the interpretation or understanding that each individual arrives at for himself from his study of its teachings. While the former is confined to the Guardian, the latter, according to the guidance given to us by the Guardian himself, should by no means be suppressed. In fact such individual interpretation is considered the fruit of man's rational power and conducive to a better understanding of the teachings,

provided that no disputes or arguments arise among the friends and the individual himself understands and makes it clear that his views are merely his own."

(From a letter of the Universal House of Justice to an individual believer, May 27, 1966; reprinted in *Lights of Guidance*, #1052, p. 311)

With this in mind, I express my thoughts in the hope that doing so will encourage others to read the *Kitáb-i-Íqán* and reap the great benefit that I have obtained from so doing.

In truth I would not have gleaned much from the *Kitáb-i-Íqán* the first time I read through it were it not for three words that stuck in my mind, begging for an explanation. Over the years I came to appreciate the value of Bahá'u'lláh's explanations of these terms and others, so much so that today I hold the discovery of their meanings dear to my heart. It was my first true experience with the Writings of Bahá'u'lláh. Today my journey continues, and I invite you to join me on this road. Naturally you can only attain insight into the Word of God by personally reading and meditating it. For this reason I have adopted an informal, conversational style. I am not delivering a lecture ; I am only talking with a friend about some discoveries that I have made. I hold this as my most humble contribution to sharing my thoughts with others, either of my faith or otherwise, and hope this will make sense to them in some way. In my thinking, learning about God, and indeed myself, His image in an eventual hoped for realization,takes an eternal journey that to me seems endless, as He is the Eternal, Unknowable Essence of Essences and I the human am created in that Image.. It requires that I have an understanding of what the Cause of Bahá'u'lláh instructs. Pen in hand then, I commit my thoughts to paper and hopefully to hearts of others.

Introduction

The *Kitab-i-Iqan* challenges the reader to immerse oneself below its surface. Words that may seem simple and easy to digest prove, upon careful reflection, to harbor deeper meaning. These are, after all, the words of a Manifestation of God revealed directly by Him and not passed through an intermediary. One has to recall that according to recorded Bahá'í History, the Book was written by the Manifestation in a period of two days and two nights, by Himself. (Taherzadeh, A, Revelation of Baha'ullah, Vol I., chapter on Kitab'i'Iqan).

Excepting only the Qur'án in known past ages the words of the Manifestation were recorded years or decades after They lived in this world. While this does not diminish the value of the Scriptures and traditions of the religions of the past, many today nevertheless doubt their authenticity and accuracy. In the case of Bahá'u'lláh's works, we can dispense with such objections. We know what He wrote. Moreover, He told us that the Word of God contains layers upon layers of meaning that can only be unfolded through sincere reflection and meditation. These are words intended to guide generations.

The *Kitab-i-Iqan* was written in Persian and Arabic.

In addition to the usual problems of translation, another presents itself. It was common among writers in those languages to encode meaning, not only through words but through numerical systems one of which is said to be known as *Abjad* assigned numbers to letters, and through them to words, and then created associations between those words and concepts based on those numbers. In what follows, I will not attempt to deal with this subject. For one thing, we will be using the English translation and not the original language. For another it is enough for most of us, at least at the outset, to consider only those meanings conveyed by the words themselves. Bahá'ís are prohibited from merely using numbers to explain scriptural meaning, but to adhere to logical proof and scientifically proven methods as well as scriptural prophecy. Our Creator did not send His Manifestations to confuse and befuddle us, but rather to guide and educate us. Although His Word is deep, we can begin by wading into the shallows and each may progress into the water at our own pace, with of course His assistance in prayer, for one has to depend on Him to reveal all hidden meanings that one can understand in the Scriptures, this accompanied by deeds of true faith in action.. This aligns such an investigation with science and logic, so that we learn the most basic truths about our world first and build upon them to reach successively greater heights of knowledge. By so doing the principle of the Bahá'í Faith, that religion, science and reason must agree is fully vindicated.

1751. Numerology

"...it is absolutely essential that the teachings should not be confused with the obscure ideas related to numerology and astrology and the like. Individuals interested in them are free to believe in and credit such ideas and to make any inferences and deductions they desire from them, but under no circumstances are they expected to identify them with the principles and teachings of the Cause. We must at this stage preserve the purity and sanctity of the Bahá'í teachings. I will pray that you may be guided in your efforts, and may succeed in safeguarding and promoting the interests of our beloved Faith."

(Ibid,. December 26, 1928, p. 9)

(Compilations, Lights of Guidance, p. 516)

It is worth noting in this connection, that the *Kitáb-i-Íqán* began with a set of questions posed to Bahá'u'lláh by one of the Báb's maternal uncles. Bahá'u'lláh fully answered those questions, but in so doing went far beyond them in such a manner that will resonate across the centuries and guide generations yet unborn. We will look at those origins in the course of this exploration. In the meantime let us simply note that Bahá'u'lláh's call for unity in diversity encompasses the whole world, not only by way of calling into being something new, but also by way of reminding us of what has always been found. After all, whether you say "Shalom Alechem," "Salaam Alaikum," "Pax Vobis Cum," or "Uxolo Malube Nani,", or "Peace be with you," you are saying the same thing.

Illustrations

A Supplication

As a token of gratitude and in remembrance of the long and turbulent spiritual path I have walked, I wish to offer a prayer that my spiritual mother Rosemary Sala taught me in Summerstrand, Port Elizabeth, South Africa a long time ago in 1961. I have kept this prayer in my heart throughout my life and hope that it will help me in my efforts to teach my Faith. Should you journey with me on this road, I hope it will be of value to you as well. The reader should note that this prayer is no longer included in authorized editions of Bahá'í prayer books.

Glory be unto Thee, O God, for Thy Manifestation of Love to mankind! O Thou, who art our Life and Light, guide Thy servants to Thy Way, and make them rich in Thee and free from all save Thee.

O God, teach them Thy Oneness, and give unto them a realization of Thy Unity; that they may see no one save Thee. Thou art the Merciful and the Giver of Bounty!

O God, create in the hearts of Thy beloved the fire of Thy Love, that it may burn away the thought of everything save Thee.

Reveal unto them, O God, Thy Exalted Eternity; that Thou hast ever been and will always be, and that there is no God save Thee. Verily, in Thee will they find comfort and strength!

(Attributed to Bahá'u'lláh in *Bahá'í Scriptures*, #264, p. 184)

First Thoughts

Like all Scripture, the *Kitáb-i-Íqán* is a deep book. You'll need to read it time and again to develop an appreciation for the gems hidden within. On your first reading you may only gain an appreciation for the flow of words and sentences, and for some of their superficial meanings. Later you may analyze a passage, a sentence, or even a word to discover deeper truths. In a sense it will be like a child learning to read letters, then words composed of those letters, and finally sentences composed of those words; later the child can then perceive deeper meaning in that which is visibly written. This must be taken with the knowledge that God can guide one through shorter steps if He wills.All understanding has to depend on Him and His good pleasure.

Additionally, your perception of the Book may not be the same as someone else's. Indeed, your perception after the first reading will not be the same as after the fifth. Consider that each time you are gaining from it benefits in keeping with your needs and capacity at that point. In this, the study of the Sacred Text is a mirror of the general principle of progressive revelation.

You might initially think, as I did, that it is enough to read the Word of God as though it were like any other book, but think again. In its opening paragraphs the *Kitáb-i-Íqán* challenges us to purity and asserts that, without detachment from all save God, understanding will not follow.

Spiritual journeys often lead through curious terrain. When I began the study of the *Kitab-i-Iqan—The Book of Certitude*--I had heard the word "certitude" only once. It had surfaced in a recording called *Words for the World*, a collection of discs issued by Kelsey Records: "Ponder now… the influence of the word of God, that thou mayest turn from left side of idle fancy to the right side of certitude".[1] Later I was attracted to the "Fire Tablet" (*Bahá'í Prayers*, p. 214), which portrays the sufferings of Bahá'u'lláh in His own words. I had no further preparation for my encounter with Bahá'u'lláh's primary theological work. Your path to it may have been similar, or it may have been very different. Mine had been in strict instruction by my parents to observe the Ten Commandments in the *Bible* and keep on the 'straight path' behavior-wise, as I grew up a "server' in the Anglican church in early life.

My Initial Reading

In 1969 in Cape Town I met Majiet Noor, who had become a Bahá'í after reading the *Kitáb-i-Iqán*. He urged me to read the Book for myself.

I spent the following year traveling extensively throughout the country with my friend Lowell Johnson,

---

[1]   *Words for the World: Selections from the Bahá'í Writings with Music* was originally a series of radio spots which were later transferred to records.

and when I arrived in Johannesburg I borrowed a copy from him. I took it to Soweto (where I temporarily lived during my travels) to read. I started in the late afternoon and finished sometime in the early hours of the following morning.

Exhausted from this reading marathon, I was perplexed by some of the material I'd encountered. In my early days as a Bahá'í, I had once attempted to read *Gleanings from the Writings of Bahá'u'lláh* and got nowhere. A compilation of partial translations of many works, it left me without a solid picture of Bahá'u'lláh's teachings. But now I had a complete Book that covered so many subjects that I found myself "mute with wonder".

I could have given up right there as I had done with *Gleanings*, but it seemed a complete enough presentation that I should have been able to follow it. The problem was not the Book, it was me. When you stop reading at 3:00 A.M., many things seem unreal!

The next day I visited the Johannesburg Bahá'í Center and learned that a member of the Universal House of Justice was about to visit. I decided to ask him some questions about the Book. When I had the opportunity, my questions revolved around the meanings of certain Arabic terms: *athim* (sinner), *Zaqqum* (an evil tree in the next world), and *karim* (honorable). He suggested that I needed some background and advised me to read the Qur'án. This advice sent me spiraling through a variety of religious texts and resulted in a reexamination of what I knew of the Scriptures of the past.

A Puzzle

In the second part of the *Kitáb-i-Íqán* we find the account of a certain Hájí Mirza Karim (meaning "honorable") Khan, who had written a book titled *Guidance for the Ignorant*. Bahá'u'lláh did not read others' books, but because Karim had attacked the tenets of the Bábí Faith, His followers insisted that He make an exception. On obtaining a copy, Bahá'u'lláh remarked on the title and briefly paged through the book. He then commented:

> **And as to this man's attainments, his ignorance, understanding and belief, behold what the Book which embraceth all things hath revealed; "Verily, the tree of Zaqqum [infernal tree] shall be the food of the Athim [sinner or sinful, Qur'án 44:43-44]." And then follow certain verses, until He saith: "Taste this, for thou forsooth art the mighty Karim! [honorable, Qurán 44:49]". Consider how clearly and explicitly he hath been described in God's incorruptible Book! This man, moreover, feigning humility, hath in his own book referred to himself as the "athim servant": "Athim" in the Book of God, mighty among the common herd, "Karim" in name!**

> (Bahá'u'lláh, *Kitáb-i-Íqán*, p. 190)

The last sentence of this passage is the one that puzzled me and led me to ask questions of the Universal House of Justice member. Eventually I asked a Persian Bahá'í friend to explain. He reminded me that the man Karim used to write newspaper articles attacking the Bábí Faith. He further gave me the sentence in the original Arabic: *Karimun fel esm, Athimun fel kitab, Azizun bayn'ul an am!* Nevertheless, I did not understand what that statement really meant. I would not come to understand it for some years: (Karim), or the honorable, by name; (athimun fel kitab) sinner in the Book; (azizun baynu'l an am) mighty among the common herd.These terms did not make sense until one finds the text of the Qur'an which reads:"The Athim shall eat of the Zaqqum"…and later "Taste thou of this for thou art Karim". This was written many years before Karim existed by Muhammad!

In the early seventies, when I was traveling with Dr. Michael Walker, a Bahá'í pioneer of Australian origin, who was reading the *Kitab-i-Iqan*, I asked him to share his understanding of this passage once he reached it. After some days of travel, he told me that it sounded like a dignified joke. To my thinking, it may well be that the statement is a joke as well as a warning with serious implications. But in time I found another reasonable explanation. To understand it, more of the background is necessary:

The Báb, the Manifestation of God who heralded Bahá'u'lláh's Revelation, was Himself preceded by two teachers, Shaykh Ahmad and Siyyid Kázim, who foretold His coming. Siyyid Kázim had enumerated the qualities that would characterize the Promised One: He would be between the ages of twenty five and thirty, would refrain from smoking, would possess innate knowledge, and would be free of bodily imperfections.

Karim had previously claimed to be this Promised One, but he did not fit this list of attributes. He was obese, one-eyed, beardless, bald, and short. Nor was he a believer. After his own claim to being a manifestation was ignored, he became an enemy of the Bábís. And his name was Karim. Curiously, in Persian these seven characteristics mentioned above all begin with the letter "K". Nevertheless he was full of pride and deigned to think himself capable of guiding "the ignorant." For, he himself wrote the book "Guidance for the Ignorant".

To my thinking, Muhammad had spoken of one who would oppose the Bábí and Bahá'í Dispensations many years before even Karim (the honorable well-known man) existed and even named him as "Karim" in His Book, hence the words: "the sinner" would eat of the " evil tree" and would still be honored as a great person.

Days of the Week

Having been told to read the Qur'án, I undertook a study not just of that Holy Book but of all the Holy Books I could lay my hands on. This quest would occupy me for years. I began not with the Qur'án but with the Holy Bible, the Book I knew from my childhood. In due course I did read the Qur'án, as well as the Baghavad Gita and a book on Buddhism called "Maitreya Amit Abha has Come" and an explanatory book by Gail Woolson called " The Divine Symphony". Among the things I learned in the course of these studies was that each religion is associated with a calendar and that a common religion is one of the defining characteristics of a culture.

Until this time it had never occurred to me that calendars other than the Christian (Gregorian) calendar existed, but I had also learned of the Julian Calendar. Although it was a simple discovery, it suggested to me a deep unity among religions in spite of their superficial differences. Moreover, it indicates a "continuity" among religions: when a new religion arises and gains adherents, there are similarities that assist an easy transition from one to another.

I found the connection between religion and culture even more profound. Religion lays the moral and ethical foundations of culture, and as it turns out the most basic aspects of these foundations are the same across religions. Their differences notwithstanding, successive religions often seemed to me to build upon those that went before, thus leading towards increasing universality.

I bring up calendars and this progression because there is a symbolic relationship one that Bahá'u'lláh utilizes in His Writings. The days of the week are fundamentally the same. The sun rises and sets, and the stars spin overhead. But each day also brings unique events, such as weather, varying with the season, and so forth. We name and number the days for our convenience, but aside from the particular circumstances of any given day, Tuesday is not very different from Thursday, and March twentieth is much like September third, for on each day the sun rises and sets as usual, however, with different events occurring on each.

In that same way, religions go by different names and have differing characteristics, yet on a certain level they are all the same. Indeed, we can speak of the "sun" of a particular religion dawning on the horizon, rising to the zenith, and sinking until it sets. Following a "night" illuminated only by the moon and stars, a new "dawn" occurs as the sun reappears.

Bahá'u'lláh uses other metaphors, too. The progression of religions can be viewed as an educational process for humanity, akin to how a child learns to roll over, then sit, then crawl, then walk, and then run. Each lesson builds upon those that went before to develop our capacities. Both individually and collectively, we learn from the past—and hope to avoid the mistakes of the past in the future!

Bahá'u'lláh's calls us to awaken to the dawn of a new day, one in which all the days of the past will culminate in the recognition of mankind as one family. This new day is His Revelation. He is its sun, and his laws and teachings are the moon and stars thereof. Bahá'u'lláh explains this relationship in His Book, where we see the word "shams" (sun) we know that this refers to the " Sun of Truth" and its dawning, the coming of the Revelation by God, the Revelation of another Manifestation of the attributes and virtues of God in human form to further explain His Eternal Intent and Purpose of His Creation and the responsibilities to Him assigned to His creatures, and we are part of those creatures....

Houses of Worship

Blessed is the spot, and the house, and the place, and the city, and the heart, and the mountain, and the refuge, and the cave, and the valley, and the land, and

the sea, and the island, and the meadow where mention of God hath been made, and His praise glorified.

(*Bahá'í Prayers*, title page)

As I investigated the idea that all religions are one, I attended services in many houses of worship. I visited a synagogue on a Saturday. I heard with joy and wonder the *Addhan* chanted at a mosque. The differences between these religions made no difference in my appreciation of them. From my childhood, I recalled my tenure as a server in my church, but now I was not "serving", but only observing. Years later I served as a guide at the Bahá'í House of Worship in Wilmette, Illinois, finally acknowledging religion as a crucial force in my life. Perhaps curiously, I had served as a member of a National Spiritual Assembly long before entering a Bahá'í House of worship to pray! Thus where prayer is offered that place is blessed…

The Scriptures of these religions had each been revealed in a different language and a different script, but that was unimportant to me. Rather, I sought the truths they contained and the specific forms in which those truths were presented. In so doing, I discovered that true spirituality has but one language—service at His Threshold.

In the following pages I include some of these calendars as examples, but this cannot be the complete list, as the Blessed Beauty mentions that there were religions before these and in languages that are no longer spoken:

Examples of Today's Religious Existent Calendars on the Planet(List not exhaustive)

(All graphics in a PowerPoint Program created by the author prior to year 2000 A.D. and extracted from the Internet at that time), exclusion not intentional but by availability of graphics)

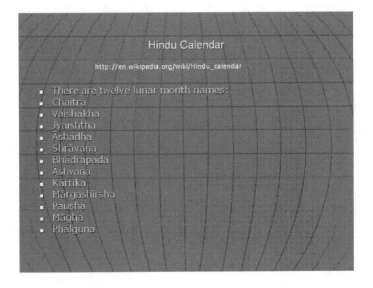

Hindu Calendar

http://en.wikipedia.org/wiki/Hindu_calendar

- There are twelve lunar month names:
- Chaitra
- Vaishakha
- Jyaishtha
- Ashadha
- Shravana
- Bhadrapada
- Ashwina
- Kartika
- Margashirsha
- Pausha
- Magha
- Phalguna

Judaism Calendar

Month	Days
Tishri	30
Heshvan	29
Kislev	29
Tevet	29
Shevat	30
Adar I	30
Adar II	29
Nisan	30
Iyar	29
Sivan	30
Tammuz	29
Av	30
Elul	29

http://webexh-bits.org/calendars/calendar-jewish.html

Festivals in Zoroastrian Calendar

http://www.avesta.org/zcal.html

- Important festivals
- Gahambars
  - Maidyozarem ('mid-spring' feast)
  - Maidyoshahem ('mid-summer' feast)
  - Paitishahem (feast of 'bringing in the harvest')
  - Ayathrem ('bringing home the herds')
  - Maidyarem ('mid-year'/winter feast)
- Hamaspathmaidyem (feast of 'All Souls')
- Noruz (New Years)
- Jashan-e Mihragan

Buddhist Calendar

Months

English name	Thai Name	Transcription
January	มกราคม	mokkarakhom
February	กุมภาพันธ์	kumphaphan
March	มีนาคม	minakhom
April	เมษายน	mesayon
May	พฤษภาคม	pruetsaphakhom
June	มิถุนายน	mithunayon
July	กรกฎาคม	karakadakhom
August	สิงหาคม	singhakhom
September	กันยายน	kanyayon
October	ตุลาคม	tulakhom
November	พฤศจิกายน	pruetsachikayon
December	ธันวาคม	thanwakhom

http://en.wikipedia.org/wiki/Thai_solar_calendar

Christian Calendar

Months With Number of Days

- 1 January 31
- 2 February 28 or 29
- 3 March 31
- 4 April 30
- 5 May 31
- 6 June 30
- 7 July 31
- 8 August 31
- 9 September 30
- 10 October 31
- 11 November 30
- 12 December 31

Islamic Calendar

- Islamic Calendar
- Muharram
- Safar
- Rabi' al-awwal
- Rabi' al-thani
- Jumada al-awwal
- Jumada al-thani
- Rajab
- Sha'aban
- Ramadan
- Shawwal
- Dhu al-Qi'dah
- Dhu al-Hijjah

http://webexhibits.org/calendars/calendar-islamic.html

Babi and Bahai Calendar

(From existing Calendar)

Bahá'í Months

Arabic Name	Translation	First Day
1st Bahá	Splendor	March 21
2nd Jalál	Glory	April 9
3rd Jamál	Beauty	April 28
4th Azamat	Grandeur	May 17
5th Nur	Light	June 5
6th Rahmat	Mercy	June 24
7th Kalimát	Words	July 13
8th Kamál	Perfection	August 1
9th Asmá'	Names	August 20
10th 'Izzat	Might	September 8
11th Mashiyyat	Will	September 27
12th 'Ilm	Knowledge	October 16
13th Qudrat	Power	November 4
14th Qawl	Speech	November 23
15th Masá'il	Questions	December 12
16th Sharaf	Honor	December 31
17th Sultán	Sovereignty	January 19
18th Mulk	Dominion	February 7

(Ayyám-i-Há Intercalary Days Feb. 26-March 1)

| 19th 'Alá' | Loftiness | March 2 * |

This Display is According to Period of
Revelation as Historically known.

Robert L. K. Mazibuko

The Translation Request

Although I did not understand much of the *Kitáb-i-Íqán* for some years, reading it in its entirety filled me with a desire to grasp some of its truths and put them into practice, scant as my ability to do so might be. Today, this Book is for me, a profound work that offers a wealth of truth. It confirmed me in the path to becoming a committed Bahá'í.

Perhaps my question prompted the National Assembly of the Bahá'ís of South and West Africa to request, (in 1972), that I translate the *Kitáb-i-Íqán* into Xhosa, an African language spoken in the Cape Province of South Africa. Alhough I completed the translation in two years, writing longhand, seven years passed before the results appeared in print. The delay came in part because I was no typist, and in part because I had a hard time deciphering my own writing! The full story of the translation can be found in my book *In Spite of All Barriers*. Regardless, at the end of the day, I had translated the *Kitáb-i-Íqán* from the Guardian's exquisite English to my rather lame Xhosa. In this effort, I was assisted by some very dedicated friends pioneering in that land at the time, and especially Dr Michael Frederick Walker, who is a Mathematician,; the English Dictionary; the Bible in Xhosa and in English; a concordance of the Bible, and a myriad of Xhosa Dictionaries.

Reading and Translating

Seeking

The Kitáb-i-Íqán opens with a call to purity. Later it addresses the qualities required of seekers after truth, and exhorts us to seek with a just and pure heart, relying upon God to aid us. Among those qualities are a prayerful attitude and purity of deeds.

I found myself simultaneously seeking and translating. The translation work put the Word of God before me, but my life was far from ideal. By the time the result was published, I was in the midst of a divorce, which made it difficult to concentrate on the work. Bahá'ís should be promoters of unity, yet here I was in one of the most divisive situations imaginable. There was little positive in my life other than the translation work itself. And yet that work proved crucial in pulling me through those difficult times, so much so that certain insights I gained at the time have remained with me over the decades. I would now like to share a few of them.

The Seal of the Prophets

Muhammad is known as "the Seal of the Prophets," a term generally understood among Muslims to mean that God will send no prophets after Him. This is a key reason why the Báb was put to death; why Bahá'u'lláh was imprisoned and exiled, and why to this day Bahá'ís are persecuted in Iran. If there can be no more prophets, anyone claiming such a station must be an imposter. End of story.

The Bahá'í understanding of this designation, however, does not preclude God from sending further Messengers. For, as Bahá'u'lláh writes, it is their belief that God will continue to send Manifestations to mankind at will in the journey of man attaining the true reason for his creation, which is no less than manifesting in himself the virtues of the Deity in his life, thereby coming close to being the intended image:

> **What outpouring flood can compare with the stream of His all-embracing grace, and what blessing can excel the evidences of so great and pervasive a mercy? There can be no doubt whatever that if for one moment the tide of His mercy and grace were to be withheld from the world, it would completely perish. For this reason, from the beginning that hath no beginning the portals of Divine mercy have been flung open to the face of all created things, and the clouds of Truth will continue**

to the end that hath no end to rain on the soil of human capacity, reality and personality their favors and bounties. Such hath been God's method continued from everlasting to everlasting.

(Gleanings from the Writings of
Bahá'u'lláh, XXVII, p. 68)

The channel through which God's grace operates is, in Bahá'í terms, the Manifestations of God. Bahá'ís count as Manifestations nine Great Religious Figures—Bahá'u'lláh, the Báb, Muhammad, Jesus, the Buddha, Moses, Abraham, Krishna, and Zoroaster—as well as others whose names are lost to history. God grants to the Manifestations the knowledge of His will, and through that knowledge the Manifestations fashion a new way of life, a new civilization, and a new era. In the time period stretching from Adam (considered representative of earlier, even prehistoric, Manifestations whose names are no longer known) to Muhammad, many prophets, both Manifestations and Seers, appeared who spoke of a Great Day, the Day of God. Bahá'ís term this period the "Adamic Cycle" or the "Prophetic Cycle." In general, the "Day of God" is the time during which the Manifestation of God dwells among us, but in this specific sense it refers to an era when humanity will become unified around a common perception of God. It is associated with the coming of the Kingdom of God on Earth the seed of which would be to Bahá'ís the establishment of the World Order of Bahá'u'lláh as indicated and explained by their Guardian Shoghi Effendi in a book of that title as above.

Bahá'u'lláh makes a clear distinction between" prophets" and "Prophets Endowed with Constancy". The Prophets " Endowed with Constancy" change many rules of existing religions, and come with a methods which we can only understand as new faiths where prophets not endowed with constancy are prophets who teach the old Faith and do not bring a new religion, but can only tell of a coming religion in the future. Thus in the Bible there is Moses Who started a religion ; Jesus Who also started a religion, but Daniel, Ezekiel, Isaiah etc. do not start new religions but can foretell of a coming Faith. They do not start a new civilization, but Those "Endowed with Constancy" do that.

The period of the Adamic Cycle is full of prophecies of a coming day. But the period after Muhammad, beginning with the coming of the Bába is to Bahá'ís a period of fulfillment of past prophecies, and not of prophesying of that Day of God. The manifestation of a system *of* administering the affairs of a community seen in the establishment by Bahá'ís of an administration with defined rules is that period of the Coming of the Kingdom, when the Will of God will be done on earth as in Heaven, a time of Justice as indicated by the Houses of Justice Bahá'ís are establishing all over the world today. Thus Muhammad becomes the Seal of the period of prophecy where the Báb begins the Era of fulfillment of past prophecies of that Day of God. This is the wish and desire of Jesus as made plain in the one prayer he revealed as a form of a hope in the future, when that Will, will be done on earth. In that sense Muhammad the Prophet seals off the Prophetic Cycle and the Báb introduces the fulfillment of all the prophecies made about that Day of God. It has to be understood that the Jews knew prayers and knew how to pray, but Jesus came and taught them what to really pray for, hope and wish for, which would be in accord with the desire of God, a world where the will of God would be done in the same way that it is done in His world in heaven. This is the reason that the Bahá'í Religion comes with a way of governance and perhaps why the second " Hidden Word" by Bahá'u'lláh is about justice, and why the governing bodies of the Faith are termed by Him " Houses of Justice". This is a huge issue, which must not to be trivialized, and made a complex situation of academic discussion which begins and ends in words. Religion is a practicality and so attaches more importance to a scientific and logical approach. Man is endowed with the mind to decipher the reasons for his creation and the Divine intention by himself and using his intellect. It is unwise to think God made all these prophecies merely to mesmerize us. They are there to make us think and look to a future and not an eternal anxiety for all. Even if we were to believe that the spheres make musical sounds as they turn, we would realize that there is happiness in creation and not just a somber reason of unhappiness. All this is made for us to feel happy when we are at the end,to meet our hearts' desire. So Bahá'ís teach that each human is endowed with the power to understand God and His religion. One has to realize that when we die we go to meet Him as alone and not with all the company we have known during our sojourn on earth. This is a reality none can escape. It is not complicated, but simple. Inasmuch as we are born, we have to die! The statement in our philosophy is:" For every being, there is a becoming". Science insists that matter cannot be created nor destroyed but can change in from. To look at this as something beyond reasoning would be foolish.

> **I was a Hidden Treasure. I wished to be made known, and thus I called creation into being in order that I might be known.**
>
> **(Bahá'u'lláh, The Kitab-i-Aqdas, p. 174).**

Besides Bahá'u'lláh makes the point that;
> **Be anxiously concerned with the needs of the age ye live in, and center your deliberations on its exigencies and requirements.**
>
> **(Gleanings from the Writings of Bahá'u'lláh, p. 213)**

Progressive Revelation

This recurring appearance of the Manifestations of God is called Progressive Revelation. Progressive Revelation is explained in the Bahá'í Writings using various images. In one sense, each Revelation is like a new day of the week. In certain respects, each new day is like those that preceded it, yet each also has unique characteristics. In another sense, each Revelation is like the springtime of a new year. We recognize the coming of spring by the signs apparent in the world: the weather turns warmer, buds swell on plants, animals return from their winter grounds or from hibernation. Just as spring brings new life to the physical world, the dawning of a new Revelation brings new spiritual life to humanity. The coming of a Manifestation of God infuses the world with fresh capacity and potential. He reaffirms the spiritual principles that underpin the religions of the past, while dispensing the remedy that the world needs at that time: new ways of understanding the divine and ourselves, and new laws.

Just as the year passes from spring to summer to autumn to winter, so religions pass through a cycle of growth and decline, after which they require renewal. Bahá'u'lláh likens the Manifestation of God to the legendary phoenix, which consumes itself in flame only to rise again from the ashes. In another sense, He describes religion like a fine robe which, although beautiful when it is new, eventually becomes outworn and needs to be replaced. The chief reason for this cycle is that humanity is constantly growing in perception of itself and the surroundings, and therefore needs further explanations of known or unknown phenomena. As with individual growth, in each age humanity as a whole has different needs, different capacities, and different problems. Some things do not change—infants and the aged both need water, both need sustenance, God and His assistance do not —but others certainly do…the times and its needs change! The needs of one time may alter from those of a subsequent age.

In addition to describing the process of progressive revelation, the *Kitáb-i-Íqán* notes that, while some are "reborn" through their encounter with the Manifestation of God, others turn against Him, ridicule Him, persecute Him and seek His death. This, too, is one of the common features of each Revelation, yet it persists in puzzling people. Indeed, this was at the heart of the questions the Báb's uncle asked Bahá'u'lláh that prompted the revelation of the Book. By way of answering, Bahá'u'lláh asks the reader to consider the past. He recounts the stories of past Manifestations of God, including Noah, Abraham, Moses, Jesus, and Muhammad among others. (One of them,, Hud, is mentioned in the Qur'án but not the Bible.) Each of these Manifestations of God faced intense opposition. Some were put to death. This happened for no other reason than that they challenged people's comfortable worldviews and taught things contrary to people's desires. Had they not done so, nobody would have opposed them. Likewise, the Báb challenged prevailing views and taught things contrary to people's desires. Thus He, too, was persecuted and put to death. Reflect upon the old stories and what is happening even now.Baháh'u'llah tells us, and it will become clear that the Day of God has dawned once more **to** fulfill all that had been promised aforetime..

Progressive revelation does not end with the Báb. At the time Bahá'u'lláh wrote the *Kitáb-i-Íqan*, He had not yet announced His Revelation. Nor does it end with Him. He foretold the coming of another Manifestation of God "after the expiration of a full thousand years," and promised that God will continue to send His Manifestations far into the future. This is His promise to us: that God will never leave us without guidance, and that whenever the robe of religion became outworn, it would be renewed.

Discovery

Religion is a part of every human culture from our earliest days to the present. Moral and behavioral standards derive from and are codified by religious beliefs, but beyond this, people have always appealed to something greater that themselves, especially in moments of danger or when hope and vision are lost. Even in polytheistic or spiritualist religions, a singular Deity often occupies the supreme position. Called by diverse names throughout the ages, this One is often perceived as being invisible to the eye yet more visible than the world itself.

The names we give to the Nameless One are legion. Sometimes we use pictures rather than words: stars of various types, the cross; a calligraphic form of the Greatest Name. Certainly there must be countless others of which we no longer know as the Blessed Beauty testifies.. Humanity's relationship with the divine crosses tens if not hundreds of thousands of years. Bahá'u'lláh notes that in the distant past religions existed of which we now have no record. In part this is because writing had not yet been developed.

> **Moreover such forms and modes of writing as are now current amongst men were unknown to the generations that were before Adam. There was even a time when men were wholly ignorant of the art of writing, and had adopted a system entirely different from the one which they now use. For a proper exposition of this an elaborate explanation would be required.**
>
> **Consider the differences that have arisen since the days of Adam. The divers and widely-known languages**

now spoken by the peoples of the earth were originally unknown, as were the varied rules and customs now prevailing amongst them. The people of those times spoke a language different from those now known. Diversities of language arose in a later age, in a land known as Bábel. It was given the name Bábel, because the term signifieth "the place where the confusion of tongues arose."

Subsequently Syriac became prominent among the existing languages. The Sacred Scriptures of former times were revealed in that tongue. Later, Abraham, the Friend of God, appeared and shed upon the world the light of Divine Revelation. The language He spoke while He crossed the Jordan became known as Hebrew (Ibrani), which meaneth "the language of the crossing." The Books of God and the Sacred Scriptures were then revealed in that tongue, and not until after a considerable lapse of time did Arabic become the language of Revelation..

(Gleanings from the Writings of Bahá'u'lláh, p. 172)

Yet life is a continuum. The past flows smoothly into the present and the present into the future. Each day we live according to our beliefs as best we can. Our beliefs may change with time and with the coming of new Revelations, but at every moment our challenge is the same. And so it is that the foundation of all religions is one. The upholding of the moral and social code of the revelation of the time, then becomes what we term religion, which by its name keeps us together.

It is worth noting that the term Qur'an means a "recital" and the Word was to be recited daily as is, many times, whereas Bayan (Discourse or Utterance), by the Báb was an explanation or "Utterance" about revelation which itself unravels the meanings in many of those Suras in the Quran. This can be compared to one of the sayings of Jesus in the Bible: "Ye cannot bear them now…"

**16:12 I have yet many things to say
unto you, but ye cannot bear them now.**

(King James Bible, John)

.Thus one finds that when one thing is taught prior to the time it becomes a reality, it makes much sense to one who has held it in the heart for long. Some things are said but matter later in life even to children, yet they are taught to hold onto them. I feel that our Creator can do that even more. Why tell Daniel of a vision occurring as a reality many centuries later? This was to Daniel a vision of the future and to us a warning of what will pertain, lest we miss to even recognize it when it does take place.

God's Way

As I worked my way through the *Kitáb[i-Íqan*, a couple of recurring themes caught my eye.

First, Bahá'u'lláh states that the coming of a Manifestation of God is heralded by signs in both the visible heaven (the visible heavens) and the invisible heaven (the spiritual realm). The former are astronomical events while the latter are teachers who herald the coming Manifestation.

He recounts that before Moses was born, Pharaoh was told of the appearance of a star heralding his fate and that of his people. Likewise, a teacher appeared among the Children of Israel who imparted news of impending salvation.

The sign in the physical heaven that heralded the birth of Jesus is well-known. The Magi followed it to Bethlehem, where they found the Christ child. Likewise, the sign in the invisible heaven was the appearance of John the Baptist, Who in this Book, Bahá'u'lláh names as Yahya (This is not surprising, knowing that the Arabic for Job is Ayyub, and Abraham, Ibrahim)., who called the people to repentance in anticipation of the coming of the Messiah.

The appearance of a star is also said to have heralded the coming of Muhammad. Likewise, a series of three teachers prepared the way for Him. Salman or Ruzbih as he is sometimes called (who would become an early follower of Muhammad) was instructed by these teachers in sequence.

Likewise, ere the beauty of Muhammad was unveiled, the signs of the visible heaven were made manifest. As to the signs of the invisible

heaven, there appeared four men who successively announced unto the people the joyful tidings of the rise of that divine Luminary. Ruz-bih, later named Salman, was honoured by being in their service. As the end of one of these approached, he would send Ruz-bih unto the other, until the fourth who, feeling his death to be nigh, addressed Ruz-bih saying: "O Ruz-bih! when thou hast taken up my body and buried it, go to Hijaz for there the Day-star of Muhammad will arise. Happy art thou, for thou shalt behold His face!"

(The Kitab-i-Iqan, p. 65)

The Báb and Bahá'u'lláh were similarly preceded by astronomical events, particularly the spectacular apparitions of Biela's Comet.

Biela's Comet, short-period <u>comet</u> named for the Austrian astronomer <u>Wilhelm, Freiherr (baron) von Biela</u> (1782–1856). It was originally discovered by French amateur astronomer Jacques Leibax Montaigne in 1772. It was rediscovered by French astronomer Jean-Louis Pons in 1805 and was identified as the 1772 comet by German mathematician <u>Carl Friedrich Gauss</u>. When it was rediscovered again *by Biela in 1826, he suggested that the comet could be the same as that of 1772 and 1805 and that it had a period of about 6.75 years. (This conclusion was independently reached both by Danish astronomer Thomas Clausen and by French astronomer Jean-Félix-Adolphe Gambart. In France the comet was called Gambart's Comet.)*

Biela's Comet underwent remarkable transformations; it was observed in 1846 to break in two, and in 1852 the fragments returned as twin comets that were never seen thereafter. In 1872 and 1885, however, when <u>Earth</u> crossed the path of the comet's known <u>orbit</u>, bright <u>meteor showers</u> (known as <u>Andromedids</u>, or Bielids) were observed, lending strength to astronomers' deduction that all <u>meteor</u> showers are composed of fragments of disintegrated comets

(Encyclopedia Brittanica)

Two teachers preceded the Báb, Shaykh Ahmad-i-Ahsai and his pupil Siyyid Kazim-i-Rashti. Siyyid Kazim would eventually sent Mullah Husayn, the Báb's first disciple, to search for the Promised One in these words:

"He then, turning his face towards his youthful disciple, Mulla Husayn-i-Bushru'i, the Babu'l-Bab,[1] addressed

him in these words: "Arise and perform this mission, for I declare you equal to this task. The Almighty will graciously assist you, and will crown your endeavours with success."

[1 He was the first to believe in the Báb, who gave him this title.]

(Shoghi Effendi, The Dawn-Breakers, p. 19)

Finally, although the Báb was a Manifestation of God, His primary mission was to prepare people for the coming of Bahá'u'lláh.

Bahá'u'lláh illustrates a second connection between the Manifestations of God: they typically appear in a guise far removed from what people expect. Moses, for example, is said to have been slow of speech or even a stutterer, yet God chose Him to speak before Pharaoh and to deliver the Jews out of bondage. Moreover, while in Egypt Moses fought with and killed a man, yet He was the One through whom the Ten Commandments were revealed. Outwardly, He was not at all the sort of man people expected God to send!

Jesus, too, was not what people expected. For one thing, the circumstances of His birth surely seemed suspicious. Although the Gospels say little about the matter other than revealing the pain and confusion Joseph initially suffered, the Qur'án also speaks of the scorn heaped upon Mary by those who knew her and her family(see Surah of Mary in Qur'an: Rodwell). Bethlehem was not a very well known town, but Jesus came from there and fulfilled that part of the Scriptures. He was of the House of David, but ruled not with the sword as King David did, but with the Word, a rule which lasted many years.. Thus that part was fulfilled too, for He definitely did say His Kingdom was not of this world, but a King of Glory He was. Had His Word held no water that Word would have died soon after His Ascension.

Muhammad had lost both parents at an early age and grew up unschooled. He was deemed ignorant and perhaps even mad. He was not anybody's idea of a Messenger of God, yet through Him the Qur'an was revealed, idolatry was supplanted, and the perpetually warring Arabian tribes were united. The very event of the coming of Muhammad preceded to huge events in the world, to which the world still clings: One was the Renaissance and the other the beginning of the Liberal and National Revolts in Europe, which resulted in creation of nationhood, a theme already begun by Islam in the creation of the state of Islam. What of the libraries we now know and medicine we now practice, one of which was in Alexandria, and the act of studying Al Jibra today's Algebra? These things do need study of origin and acknowledgement. I am Bahá'í and this does not hurt or change me at all. Also I am an African and have accepted the use of scientific items from the West without the least hurt in their use. Personally I feel these things are the wealth of humans amassed over years from diverse corners of the earth. Anyone denying this has not studied history and geography, let alone the establishment of world communities. To me that is reality! We should be thankful one to the other for what we have today in the world, and praise God for such possibilities in our lives.

The Báb was young and had very little schooling. He made his living as a merchant assisting an uncle. When He claimed to be the Qa'im, it must have seemed outrageous. He was not like the Mullas, Ulamas and Mujtahids who had studied the Quran, nor was He old enough to be respected for His experience. One of his own uncles found it hard to believe, so much so that he asked the questions that Bahá'u'lláh answered in the *Kitáb-i-Íqan*. The other maternal uncle of the Báb testified with his life to the truth of his Nephew's declaration, for he was martyred in Teheran for His Faith. Believers in the Bahá'í Faith remember so fondly those Seven Martyrs of Tehran of whom one was the uncle of the Báb, Haji Mirza Siyyid Ali. They evinced such knowledge and power that twenty thousand died for His Cause, and some Western observers commented that His life had no parallels except that of Jesus. Was not Their Ministry for a mere six years too? Were They not Both displayed in public at Their execution? Did they not summon men to God again?

Reflecting on how little the Manifestations of God meet our expectations, I thought of a verse from Isaiah:

> **For my thoughts are not your thoughts, neither are your ways my ways, saith the LORD.**
>
> (King James Bible, Isaiah 55:8)

Meditations on Various Themes

The Influence of the Word of God

Whenever a Manifestation of God comes to us, we greet Him with mockery, scorn, and violent opposition. Those in power seek to discredit and destroy Him and His followers. Yet in spite of such tribulations, their influence cannot be suppressed and the spread of their teachings cannot be stopped. In due course, civilizations are built upon their Revelations. Their coming renews humanity's spiritual life and revitalizes societies. They have talked of their Revelations in various terms: Jesus named it "the bread of life" (John 6:36) and the Bahá'í Writings speak of the return of the divine springtime. These are images of renewal and sustenance. Just as our bodies cannot live without physical sustenance, our spirits cannot live without divine sustenance.

In another sense, the coming of a Manifestation of God is judgment day...a day of reckoning. For although they call us to God, our response is often to harm the very One who has come to give us life. Individually we are each called to a reckoning at the hour of our return to God, but in the day of the Manifestation some are raised from "death" to spiritual life while others perish in the wasteland of ignorance and selfish desire. This is the "separation" often described in the Holy Books...of the sheep from the goats; of the righteous from the ungodly...performed by the "sword" of the Word of God.

God has assigned us two chief duties. The first is to recognize and believe in His Manifestations; the second is to obey His word. These duties are explicitly set forth in the Kitab-i-Aqdas, in the Epistle of James, and in other Scriptures. Good works, 'Abdu'l-Baha explains, are insufficient in absent knowledge of the meaning of good. On the other hand, claiming faith while failing to put it into practice is hypocrisy. The Báb stated that declarations of faith must be accompanied by acts of faith. In essence, faith must be proven through action, and action must be motivated by faith. Faith, in turn, is grounded in the Word of God, for without it we would not know which way to turn. Witness the turmoil in present-day society, where religion is so often cast aside and people formulate codes of ethics and morals based on their own narrow and selfish interests. The Word of God creates civilizations, refines manners, and shows humanity the path toward its destiny. The Manifestations of God reveal the principles and laws necessary to promote the peace and security of peoples and nations. Today, the focus of Revelation is the whole planet. Bahá'u'lláh has laid the foundations for a peaceful global society. But aside from its scope, this is not something unprecedented, for throughout history we see that religion, when properly followed, plays a crucial role in securing the welfare of peoples and nations.

From an individual's perspective, the Word of God is vital: it connects us with our Creator and enables our spiritual growth. It teaches us not only how to live but how to perceive. For example, human history is rife with misfortune and disaster. We might easily live our lives in fear or allow trial after trial to break our spirits. But from the Word of God we discover that this world is mere mirage which cannot appease our thirst. Though real in its own right, it is not our true home. Our true home is the realm of the spirit. We must not, therefore, cling to this limited world. Tests and trials are given us to help us become detached from all save God and to develop our spiritual capacity. Without them we would have no incentive to rise above the level of the animal.

Indeed, without the influence of the Holy Books, human existence would be lower than the animal. The animal was made for this world and needs nothing else. But if we fail to develop our spiritual nature, then we shut ourselves out from our true home. Human perfection lies in virtuous actions and in love for and obedience to God. Indeed, without such motivation, even virtuous actions are deprived of their benefit, for outwardly virtuous acts can be taken for entirely selfish motives. Looking at this in a deeper perspective, as believers we know that God knows all our actions, and not only does He know the action He is also aware of its intent and actuations. Who then do we fool when we show outward goodness and inward evil for any individual while performing any deed of 'good' for anyone? There can be no reward nor legitimate spiritual growth from God, while He knows that the action was not at all performed to please Him or in obedience to any of the Laws He instructs us to execute or obey. In fact such an act would appear to be a deception and therefore punishable.

Change and the Law

Every religion sets forth laws. The most fundamental are changeless and are restated by every Manifestation of God. Among them are truthfulness, charity, faithfulness, justice, and so forth. The basic fundamentality of spiritual laws can be made clearer in that they have the property of being non-quantifiable. None can give anyone a gallon of mercy, love or faith. These are actually qualities of godliness or qualities which in their perfection describe God Himself. It would then be obvious from the definition that God is Unknowable, that He cannot be quantified by those He created from the 'dust of the earth". We all have to admit that we, as bodies, are processed and reprocessed by the earth we live on. Any doubt of this would have to reflect on why vegetables come from the ground we are buried in after we eat sheep and vegetables. It would seem that God will assign a soul to a union that has been making a request in the legitimate way He has given us. Why these actions sometimes are not according to His law and yet made firm, might be because He allows us to live under His sun without making it any cloudier for any individual just because they do not believe in Him. He waits and waits with great patience, lest we change our minds and obey. It is His creation and it goes nowhere without His willing it. All actions return to Him:

There is none other God besides Him. His is all creation and its empire. All stands revealed before Him; all is recorded in His holy and hidden Tablets

(Gleanings from the Writings of
Bahá'u'lláh, p. 149)

These laws might be called spiritual laws. In addition, religions set forth laws regulating forms of worship and such social matters as marriage and divorce, the conduct of business, and burial rites. These laws change from one Dispensation to the next for they are for a safety for a time and not as fundamental as spiritual laws which are based on a deeper behavioral system that responds deeply to His law. In most cases the very individual would know whether they break the law or not and not one outside that one person executing the action.. These changes have to do with changing social conditions. Such laws are thus custom-made to serve the needs and capacities of people living in widely disparate times.

But there are other changes in religious laws which seem to have a very different purpose. In the *Kitáb-i-Iqán*, Bahá'u'lláh offers an example. During their daily prayers, Muslims face a particular point on the Earth's surface known as the Qiblih (the Point of Adoration). Since the days of Muhammad, the Qiblih has been the temple in Mecca known as the Kaaba. According to tradition the Kaaba was built by Adam. Later it fell into ruin and was rebuilt by Abraham, assisted by his son Ishmael. (Faizi, *The Prince of Martyrs*, p. 6.) Within it, Abraham placed the Black Stone, said to have been carried to him from Paradise by the angel

Gabriel (Balyuzi, *Muhammad and the Course of Islam*, p.18). This is the stone Muslims kiss during their pilgrimage. The color of the stone is said to have changed color from being kissed in adoration through the ages.

But it was not always so since originally, Muhammad and His followers turned to Jerusalem during prayer. One day this suddenly changed. Bahá'u'lláh recounts the tale thus:

> **And likewise, reflect upon the revealed verse concerning the "Qiblih." When Muhammad, the Sun of Prophethood, had fled from the dayspring of Batha unto Yathrib, He continued to turn His face, while praying, unto Jerusalem, the holy city, until the time when the Jews began to utter unseemly words against Him -- words which if mentioned would ill befit these pages and would weary the reader. Muhammad strongly resented these words. Whilst, wrapt in meditation and wonder, He was gazing toward heaven, He heard the kindly Voice of Gabriel, saying: "We behold Thee from above, turning Thy face to heaven; but We will have Thee turn to a Qiblih which shall please Thee." On a subsequent day, when the Prophet, together with His companions, was offering the noontide prayer, and had already performed two of the prescribed**

Rik'ats, the Voice of Gabriel was heard again: "Turn Thou Thy face towards the sacred Mosque." In the midst of that same prayer, Muhammad suddenly turned His face away from Jerusalem and faced the Ka'bih. Whereupon, a profound dismay seized suddenly the companions of the Prophet. Their faith was shaken severely. So great was their alarm, that many of them, discontinuing their prayer, apostatized their faith. Verily, God caused not this turmoil but to test and prove His servants. Otherwise, He, the ideal King, could easily have left the Qiblih unchanged, and could have caused Jerusalem to remain the Point of Adoration unto His Dispensation, thereby withholding not from that holy city the distinction of acceptance which had been conferred upon it.

(Kitab-i-Iqa, p. 50-51)

Even as He hath revealed: "The East and West are God's: therefore whichever way ye turn, there is the face of God."

(The Kitab-i-Iqan, p. 51)

Change, especially change in deeply-rooted patterns of life, challenges us. But when something we associate with God's law changes, we often rebel at the thought. Yet surely God has the power and authority to decree what He wills! So changes of this sort are, Bahá'u'lláh affirms, to test our faith.

During the Dispensation of Bahá'u'lláh, the Qiblih changed again and is now the place where His earthly remains are buried—Bahji, in Israel, where Bahá'ís travel on pilgrimage.

The Sun, the Moon, the Stars

As I considered the Day of Judgment, it struck me that much of what has been said on the subject had to be metaphorical. For example, the Gospel of Mark records Jesus' words:

> **But in those days, after that tribulation, the sun shall be darkened, and the moon shall not give her light, and the stars of heaven shall fall, and the powers that are in heaven shall be shaken. And then shall they see the Son of man coming in the clouds with great power and glory."**
>
> (Mk 13:24-26, KJV; compare also Mt 24:29-30)

How should this be understood? If the sun stopped shining, all life on Earth would be extinguished. Are eclipses intended? Surely not, for they are too common and do not affect the whole of the Earth. Falling stars could suggest a meteor shower, but again these happen regularly year after year. And no star could literally collide with the Earth without the Earth being completely destroyed!

In the *Kitáb-i-Íqán*, Bahá'u'lláh offers a different sort of explanation: By the sun, moon, and stars are meant spiritual luminaries, leaders of religion. For centuries their "light" illuminates humanity, but prior to the Day of Judgment they "grow dark" and "fall." That is, they cease to offer true guidance and illumination, and descend into ignorance and corruption. The result is darkness upon darkness, for souls seeking enlightenment have nowhere to turn for guidance.

Bahá'u'lláh gives a second interpretation, as well. The sun, moon and stars can also be viewed as the laws of the previous dispensation which, due to the passage of time, are no longer sufficient for prevailing circumstances. Because of this, their "light" been extinguished. It is painfully obvious that without the persons who are regarded as leaders in spirituality, keeping up that standard to the best of their ability,, those who look up to them will certainly fall when they fall. Thus will the moons that reflect divine guidance be the sources of darkness upon darkness, and thus, those who fashion their lives after them, the stars of that heaven, fall too. Jesus has mentioned that we should be like a light on a mountain in holding up that standard that others may see this success in such a difficult path and attempt to emulate that example,without which they would proBábly fail. A spiritually alert person should know that such a position is the envy of many and they look to them to keep up the teaching. We know that Jesus also speaks of believers as being the salt of the world. It is the salt that makes the food tasty. Thus they are beloved of God, for they are pleasing unto Him. There are then very few of them. With Jesus there were only eleven, and one never does expect the salt to be too much!

> **Thus, by the "sun" in one sense is meant those Suns of Truth Who rise from the dayspring of ancient glory, and fill the world with a liberal effusion of grace from on high. These Suns of Truth are the universal Manifestations of God in the worlds of His attributes and names.**
>
> **(The Kitab-i-Iqan, p. 32)**

> **In another sense, by the terms 'sun', 'moon', and 'stars' are meant such laws and teachings as have been established and proclaimed in every Dispensation, such as the laws of prayer and fasting**
>
> **(The Kitab-i-Iqan, p. 38)**

Becoming a True Seeker

Bahá'u'lláh devotes several pages of the *Kitáb-i-Íqan* to establishing the requirements for seeking God and His Cause. This is a remarkable passage in this Book, because it suggests that one must attain a high degree of virtue to be a true seeker. On first reading it sounds as though one must be very spiritually pure to seek that path to God. How could that be? In this regard I would think it necessary to make every effort one can to please God with whatever one knows will please Him, in the hope that he will assist that believer in Him to attain more knowledge about Himself. After all he knows the way and He wants us to strive to find it, while loving Him. Hence that love would tend to seek His help and presence at all times during that journey, for endless it is. To seek as an image to emulate the essence has to be hard, given the incapability and failures of the flesh. At times during that search which can be hard, I find it necessary to appeal to Him in such words as: " You want me to pass this test and You know it is hard. If You want me to pass, kindly assist me.. I know not the way. In those cases the words " Quo Vadis " do amply apply. For, one never knows where the road leads and we travel it once and hope we do so, in safety.

We have remember that God is Unknowable. That is, the human mind is incapable of comprehending its Creator. At best, it can know itself and the words are: **" He knows God, who knows himself".** But then, who can say they know themselves that well?

> **O My servants! Could ye apprehend with what wonders of My munificence and bounty I have willed to entrust your souls, ye would, of a truth, rid yourselves of attachment to all created things, and would gain a true knowledge of your own**

selves -- a knowledge which is the same as the comprehension of Mine own Being. Ye would find yourselves independent of all else but Me, and would perceive, with your inner and outer eye, and as manifest as the revelation of My effulgent Name, the seas of My loving-kindness and bounty moving within you.

(Gleanings from the Writings of Bahá'u'lláh, p. 326)

He Who is the eternal King -- may the souls of all that dwell within the mystic Tabernacle be a sacrifice unto Him -- hath spoken: "He hath known God who hath known himself."

(Gleanings from the Writings of Bahá'u'lláh, p. 178)

Even the Manifestations of God confess their inability to comprehend God and their nothingness before Him. In this sense, to seek God is never to find Him, but rather to draw ever closer to Him and through His Manifestation. Jesus has identified that station as being that of coming to the Father through Himself and one cannot draw closer to Him without loving Him and following His precepts. Being a true seeker is therefore a commitment to transformation.

Bahá'u'lláh draws a parallel between spiritual transformation and material transformation:

> **Consider the doubts which they who have joined partners with God have instilled into the hearts of the people of this land. "Is it ever possible," they ask, "for copper to be transmuted into gold?" Say, Yes, by my Lord, it is possible. Its secret, however, lieth hidden in Our Knowledge. We will reveal it unto whom We will. Whoso doubteth Our power, let him ask the Lord his God, that He may disclose unto him the secret, and assure him of its truth. That copper can be turned into gold is in itself sufficient proof that gold can, in like manner, be transmuted into copper, if they be of them that can apprehend this truth. Every mineral can be made to acquire the density, form, and substance of each and every other mineral. The knowledge thereof is with Us in the Hidden Book.**

> **(Gleanings from the Writings of Bahá'u'lláh, XCVII, p. 197)**

Should such a transformation occur, would it be possible, Bahá'u'lláh asks, to say that the newly-formed gold was still copper? Clearly not. Likewise, spiritual transformation is a firm reality and God can confer it on anyone who testifies truly to His existence by affirming the Authority of His Manifestation. In that regard, one may wish to meditate on the crimes of the thief crucified with Jesus, for he was promised immediate association in the Next World, though this was not really the course of his past life. This brings out the case of not focusing on the sins of others, for in death they might do something that causes them to attain Paradise, more than a person, holy in life, but found by death in an evil state, thus forfeiting much.Through it, the old person, steeped in ignorance and sin, is "reborn" and becomes a new person, attracted to God and seeking His light. Although there is no end to spiritual growth, the moment of transformation effectively creates something new that wasn't there before.

> **23:39 And one of the malefactors which were hanged railed on him, saying, If thou be Christ, save thyself and us.**
>
> **23:40 But the other answering rebuked him, saying, Dost not thou fear God, seeing thou art in the same condemnation? 23:41 And we indeed justly; for we receive the due reward of our deeds: but this man hath done nothing amiss.**
>
> **23:42 And he said unto Jesus, Lord, remember me when thou comest into thy kingdom.**
>
> **23:43 And Jesus said unto him, Verily I say unto thee, To day shalt thou be with me in paradise.**
>
> **(Luke, Holy Bible)**

A thief dying for his crimes is, in a moment, transformed into a follower of Christ and is promised Paradise, not in a few days, not in a week, not in a thousand years, but that very day. This is real transformation, real rebirth. Bahá'u'lláh, too, says that such transformation can occur in a moment.

Being a true seeker is therefore not merely about trying to find God, but about growing in His light. It means casting away all other aspirations and seeking God solely out of love for Him. It is not even about attaining to Paradise. As the Báb wrote,

> **"Worship thou God in such wise that if thy worship lead thee to the fire, no alteration in thine adoration would be produced, and so likewise if thy recompense should be paradise. Thus and thus alone should be the worship which befitteth the one True God.**
>
> **(The Persian Bayán, VII, 19.** *Selections from the Writings of the Báb,* **p. 77)**

Paradise is a creation of God. To desire it rather than Him is to place it above Him or make it His partner on par, or even, to make it our God. We should worship God with neither expectation of reward nor fear of punishment, but solely out of love for our God and Creator

Miracles

The Holy Books and traditions of many religions recount tales of miracles performed by God's prophets and

Messengers. Some people hold that these miracles are proofs that these prophets and Messengers sent were from God. Clearly miraculous works are not a definitive proof that a person was sent from God. As proofs of being prophet, miracles do not work. Anyone can claim they saw a miracle, but only those who actually did see it can be sure, and even then the senses are easily fooled. Stage magicians manufacture "miracles" all the time as entertainment. We all know nothing miraculous is actually happening, but we love to be dazzled in this way. The possibility that something truly miraculous has happened thrills us even more.

The Manifestations of God certainly have the power to work miracles, and they may do so out of their love and compassion for others. But they did not come to entertain us. They do not wish us to be "wowed" by their powers, nor do they regard miracles as having any particular importance as proofs. They come to educate us and guide us and uplift us. If we need proof of their stations, we do not need miracles. We only need consider their lives, their teachings, and their effect upon the world. Do they sacrifice their all for us? Do they transform ignorance and nonbelief into knowledge and faith? Do they guide the sinner into righteousness? Do they, over the course of time, fundamentally alter the course of history?

Consider that Jesus died on the cross with but a handful of faithful followers gathered to Him, all of who on that day were broken in spirit, yet in time Christianity encompassed nearly the entire world. Consider that Bahá'u'lláh, an exile and a prisoner, has already called into being a worldwide community of followers that is one of the most diverse groups of people ever seen. These are the true miracles, the miracles of lasting importance for humanity as a whole.

So if the miracles of God's Messengers are not proof, what are they? To a larger sense they are metaphors. Let a physically blind man be given physical sight and he will see for a time, until his death. Let a physically ill woman be healed, and she will be healthy until another illness overtakes her. Although compassionate, these are things of limited duration and value. But let the spiritually blind be given sight, let the spiritually sick be healed, let the spiritually dead be awakened to new life, and these things will follow them through eternity. Stories of physical miracles serve as metaphors to teach us about spiritual reality. It is certain that they prove that Manifestations are in command of the creation but are by themselves no entire proof of Their coming from God.

We live in an age of rationality, where people demand concrete evidence and solid proofs. The very idea of miracles is often mocked. Many are repelled from religion because they see it as magical thinking or as unsubstantiated claims of impossible happenings. This is no doubt a key reason why the miraculous is not given as evidence of the truth in the Bahá'í Faith. People need better reasons than unverifiable stories of the miraculous to ground their beliefs. At the same time, the symbolism inherent in stories of miracles has great value, and we can see the logic in such stories when we view them not as the theme but symbolism of a teaching.. We do not need to deny that the miracles might have happened. They might have. But we should recognize that whatever they are, they are not proofs. Rather, the Manifestations of God are, Themselves, their own greatest proofs.

The origins in the earthly life of all the Manifestations are a miraculous event. For They seemingly come from nowhere or very humble backgrounds but establish faiths that last centuries.

It is my contention that Jesus did not feel the pain of the cross as much as we make out that He did. When He was threatened with being stoned, He escaped because His work was not yet complete at that stage. When He was ready He walked into Jerusalem at Passover, knowing exactly what He was walking into, for He warned His followers of the event. I would think that He wanted nobody to claim that they forgot His teaching, and so allowed them to hang Him in order to deliver His last and lasting Sermon which we remember today after so many years and remember why He had to sacrifice His life. To Him it was a return Journey to the Father, but He had to choose a method of teaching even in death. It was His aim to die on the cross. Why return to Jerusalem when all the rabbis who did not like His teachings would be there? He was establishing new laws, Why then celebrate Passover? This to me was the most public declaration of His faith, an unforgettable one.

It took seven hundred and fifty soldiers to kill the Báb. That was public enough, not to be forgotten. He had done His job and well.

Bahá'u'lláh, a Prisoner of two Kings (Iran and Turkey) wrote from Prison and even had some of His followers attain martyrdom, for He knew they would meet later, and gave them that assurance. The one huge miracle is that a Cause which started with twenty young people in Iran(Even though there were first Eighteen Letters of the Living, the Báb addressed His twenty Tablets to the Letters of the Living, and that seemed to include Himself and Him Whom God Shall Make Manifest, the latter statement is my surmise. The Tablets appear in the book "The Dawn-Breakers") is now celebrated all over the world because of the need to adjust the world to a new era it is on the brink of. Have we not just gone to the Moon? Does that not redefine all we knew before.? Is that not why the world is in turmoil, because it really has no basis of what happens next? The scare of teleology is in our hearts, when belief in God says: God is the King and has manifested One Who says we shall see this through if we do certain things the right way. If we do not do those things, we do not even know if that is a guarantee that they shall never occur and without us in the effort. Shall we then have failed to respond?

A Faith of twenty is now in languages as many more as that and in many countries. That is one miracle, that the Prisoner did this!

If God were to send His angels in their form, none would say: "yay or nay". It would be too scary. God wants us to think and so send one who speaks our language, who eats with us, and mentions all these things at the very risk of being done in by us the recipients of so great a mercy. It is a very grave demonstration that Sodom and Gomorrah are no longer there. It shows that we do not and never did own this place.

All expect the same miracle of God, as if He is not the Very Designer of so Complex a Universe that we hang on a piece of dust in it, and are made of that dust in bodies, but are promised greater life if we take up certain behaviors. This seems to have been in each era: The threat, the promise. Attainment of virtues that defy definition, but are linked together, seems to be the answer, for they are not defined by time and era but are there always as a standard of faith. The miracle of the reality of where we are, never dawns on us at all. For we know not the place we are in, but must live on in the hope and faith of promises from Wise Men and Women, Who come in Every Era with things we first abhor before we accept them in earnest disregarding all safety in doing so, for they are life!

The Role of God's Manifestations

The Manifestations of God come to us from God, invested with power and authority given them by God. Although they may be persecuted on Earth, their influence endures and grows for centuries. Entire civilizations rest upon their teachings. At certain times they speak with the Voice of God, as though God Himself were among us. At other times they speak as humble servants, as though they were men like any other. But in all cases, they are conveying God's Message and do His Will.

Jesus, for example said that He was with the Father and the Father was in Him. In the Qur'an, Muhammad states that He was not the father of anyone, but was the prophet of God (Sura 33:40), yet everyone knew His daughter was Fatimih. Such statements are made from specific points of view: the unity of Christ with God, the station of Muhammad as God's Prophet. Bahá'u'lláh speaks sometimes as God Himself and other times as a lowly servant.

Yet all of God's Manifestations speak of God as being far above the reach and conception of His servants, and all testify to their servitude before God. Moreover they regard

Themselves as one in spite of their outward differences. Each Manifestation of God is entrusted with a specific Mission and given a specific Message, suited to the needs and capacities of the people to whom they are sent. Otherwise they are all the true Kings of Existence... the embodiments of the Word of God itself. They are the vital link connecting three fundamental realms of existence: the world of God, the world of the Manifestations, and the world of the servants.

Like divine physicians, the Manifestations take the pulse of the world, that is, perceive the problems manifest in the world in their day, and in a wise method,prescribe a remedy for all those sicknesses they have perceived, In order to achieve this, They are prepared to suffer any injustice, for their Lives are so exalted that this world to them appears like a grain of dust in the hand of the Creator, a mere mirage that satisfies no thirst. . but perceived it as the wise creation of One that sends them, before Whom they confess to being lost in darkness as the most abject servants before His threshold. One doubting this has just to read a volume of Bahá'u'lláh supplications called " Prayers and Meditations of Bahá'u'lláh." They cannot show us all they can do, because they each have a message for a time and stand humbly at the Door of the Creator, the Source of Their Message and Their Joy and Hope, The One Who Sends Them out to teach His Cause, at a certain time, with certain problems to attend to. Thus Christ mentions the many things he could tell, but regrets that we cannot stand them at that time. However, He promises a future telling by Someone Else, Whom He names " The Sprit of Truth". Thus He even says:" Before Abraham was, I am." Remember His statement: " I am". For, the Manifestation has ever been the Messenger to humankind or beings of God, whatever language or tribe or station in life He might want to conveniently take up to deliver the message He has been given to deliver... The son-ship, the prophet-hood, the friendship, the builder of the ark of salvation, the stutterer and interlocutor savior ... all are part of that convenience which itself is a lesson to us.

Some have described the Manifestations in many derogatory terms, and it grieves one to know that They came to give a hand to the progress of humankind, at a time humankind was immersed n a state of dangerous extinguishing the light of religion among themselves.

I have heard some even speak of Muhammad as a "dangerous " Person... ignoring the influence His teaching had in the Arabian and even the European area, for, from Him and His religion came out medical teachings and libraries, at a time when the arts grew fabulously. We see this and never think why it happened. It is not just the followers we should look at, but the teaching itself in the right place at the right time in history and with the right attitude of those who placed it there.

War was deemed necessary by humans for years. Even King David(the writer of all the Psalms) was instructed by God to be a fighter, which is announced as a reason that God did not choose him to build His House. His was to fight for the space, and for Solomon who desired wisdom to build a House to Worship Him.

Muhammad came at a time when it was necessary to fight for space. Indeed even the liberal and national revolts were some of a result of that notion. However, the national revolts themselves served Muhammad's purpose of starting the formations of nations, as the nation of Islam became a healthy notion for the Middle East and the Europe of that time.. Today Bahá'u'lláh had prohibited fighting for space or for a religion and deems service to His Cause the main issue, even if that service meant execution. After all, are we not all to return to God eventually? What if we passed from this world in the shame of having done nothing for anybody except ourselves? Muhammad died or ascended as a fighter for the space to be occupied by those who were prepared to be united enough to form states, which would model what we have today as our systems. Is not our very theme of mathematics based on Arabic and Hindu numbers? Or can we deny that too? Let every man place himself in the situation of another,understand it, and then state how they would have acted differently... then they should ask themselves why they never did that in the first place and allow it to come to the state it in now. We still have our wars over space and property, and Bahá'u'lláh says that is antiquated that this is the time for thinking about uniting the planet, so that we can face all future as a united people, diverse and mixed in color as it will soon be the case.

Who is to say of what origin in that state and time one is? We are faced with a crisis of being what we have to be,and we face it with much trepidation, for the great fear is to be swallowed up when we already are mixed in our origins anyway we look at it! It would not surprise me for a black mother to give birth t o a white child in the mixture of genes we have had in our past. Who is to say which will be dominant, and at what time? I fear for the accusation such a mother will bear! It is not a case of "wait and see" but one of "prepare for the unknown that is to come!"

The words of the Báb at the end of His address in 1844

in Shiraz given to seventeen men and a woman(In the "Dawn_Breakers, Tahrih the eiteenth letter of the living declared her faith in absentia, having had a vision of One in Prayer and was recognized by the Báb as one of the eighteen first believers in Him) who were to face a very hard time even death for most, for teaching a faith:

> **Arise in His name, put your trust wholly in Him, and be assured of ultimate victory.**
>
> **(The Dawn-Breakers, p. 94)**

Returning

Every religion has some kind of "return" prophecy, and generally people take these prophecies literally. The Jews expected Elijah to return before the Messiah appeared. Christians expect Jesus to return. Shi'ih Islam looks forward to the return of the twelfth Imam. Bahá'u'lláh, however, states that such prophecies refer not to the return of the same individual, but the return of the spirit of the former Prophet and the qualities that are associated with Him.

The idea is expressed in metaphors. Consider the turning of the years... each year spring is followed by summer, then autumn, then winter, after which spring "returns." Each springtime is the return of the previous, although each springtime has its own distinctive characteristics.

Or consider the harvests of apples gathered year after year. The apples picked last year and those picked this year are the same in color, taste, and texture. They can be considered one and the same. Again, the days of the week are all the same, although each goes by a different name and the actual events of each will be different. But all have the same duration: one rotation of the Earth upon its axis. Likewise, each Manifestation brings a specific Message, yet they share deep commonalities. All come from one God, all possess all perfections (whether or not they outwardly manifest them), and each will be opposed by the very people who purport to believe in God because the Message brought is not always in accordance with man's wishes, nor can its future be seen by man in the distance. Man travels a road he has not known but which is known to His Creator, the Knower of Things Unseen..

Each day the sun rises, climbs to the zenith, declines, and then sets. Thus it is with religions. Each rises until it attains its full influence, then gradually declines and loses its influence. In due course, God sends His Manifestation to renew our faith and provide for the next stage in our collective growth. This succession of religions is not because God in competition with Himself, but rather is a necesssity for the development of humanity.

Although the Manifestations exhibit the attributes of God and are one with Him, He remains the Unknowable Essence. He no more literally descends to Earth than the sun does, yet His bounties and bestowals continually rain down upon us, just as the sun's radiance continually bathes the Earth. The coming of a Manifestation of God is like the sunrise, the return of the daytime after the darkness of night. It is the same sun that rises each morning, even though it rises from different points on the horizon and even though each day has its own name. It should be clear to the reader that we as servants of the Divine Being, must not, and indeed do not fabricate prophecies, neither, when they have been stated by authoritative persons, who over time, have proved their reliability, fulfill them ourselves. They are fulfilled by the Word revealed from On High, and by a Supreme Being, Who holds sway over all revelation to us, of Himself, always excusing the pronoun of convenience we use. It is He Who revels Himself, when He wills of His Own. As the Báb in the same address above states, that no one knows Him, the Father of Heaven, Who is stated to hold all dominion in His Hand, a theme clearly and firmly expressed by Bahá'u'lláh in His Writings, cases which number a myriad times in number..

The Bábís

When Bahá'u'lláh returned from his mountain retreat Sar-Galu near the town of Sulaymaniyyih in Ottoman-ruled Kurdistan, His first task was to renew the character of the Bábí community. He had left that community to live in the wilderness for those two years because, first, it is clear to me that He had a task which none could even understand ; secondly, because there were many misconceptions that the Bábís had about the Revelation that was to follow, nor had some of them totally grasped the meaning of the Call of the Báb. Thus there had been some confusion about what to do after the martyrdom of the Báb, a confusion that led to the loss of most of the spirit of what He stood for. The result had been a reason to the friends to go back to old ways, much as the Israelis desired to return to Egypt after the rigors of the desert they travelled. Some of the Bábís had even claimed leadership of the group without any convincing proofs. Bahá'u'lláh,not wishing to be part of the controversy that followed, as was the case of the Ascent of Muhammad and what followed, left the group for a period of two years, with no intention to return. Until forced by circumstance of feelings, thoughts and meditations as well as events that seemed to be beyond His control, He then returned to the group to assist them. This makes it clear that He had no desire for leadership about teaching the religion of God but would obey the injunction to teach it, divorcing Himself from any will of His own in that obedience. This stands clear in His deeds and words. To that end, He revealed several tablets as well as *The Hidden Words*, and the *Kitáb-i-Íqán* shortly after His return. These works were directly received by the Bábís themselves, not the wider world, and helped them to understand the new Revelation. In them, Bahá'u'lláh did not directly address His own station, which He would only reveal years later on the eve of His departure from Baghdad.

Bahá'u'lláh, however, was not the head of the Bábí community. The Báb had given that role to Mirza Yahyá, a younger half-brother of Bahá'u'lláh for His father who was Islamic could have more than one wife according that Faith. To go into that question would be another long story, just as it would be to explain the Law of Moses of an eye for an eye, one may wish to seek sources for that and is very much encouraged by the writer to do so freely and truthfully, with a great measure of honesty for the law of God is a Law and has reasons, some for a period in life and are meant to be a protection to His creature man. In all religions, moral law is present and does not change, where social laws, which seem to be influenced by time and circumstance do change. It would be wise to seek answers also to why Jesus had to be circumcised. The answer being that it was an accepted law of the day. Some issues in history and culture need one to place one's self within the circumstance of the day it which the law was promulgated. This short explanation is merely intended to prove that nothing was hidden in Bahá'í history such that we do not know about it.

Named by the Báb, Subh-i-Azal (Morning of Eternity), Mirza Yahyá was to guide the Bábi community until the time when "He Whom God shall make Manifest" arose.

Concerning the term assigned by the Báb to Mirza Yahya,, Bahá'u'lláh is said to have revealed a text mentioned by Adib Taherzadeh in hs book. Adib was a member of the Universal House of Justice before His passing, and served as one of the Continental Board of Counselors of the Faith for a while, before election. Such a station in the Cause was meant to help in the duties of the Hands of the Cause who were diminishing through passing on, at that time, such that in time there would be none left and their duties had to be assigned to another institution of the Faith to perform, as was the case, in 1968 when this was done.. Adib is a Bahá'í historian and wrote over four volumes of the Faith and its early history in his lifetime. So the testimony he gives in this case is true even if the actual text is not at this time quoted. One would remember that not all Bahá'í Writings have yet been translated from the Persian and Arabic, yet we find difficulty with what we already have. The Bahá'í Religion has to last many centuries before another Manifestation comes. This text can be found in Bahá'í Writings: Besides the behavior of Mirza Yahya does not endear him to any believer in the truth of the Faith. This is plainly recorded in many books and is not contested.

In my thinking, this the naming of Mirza Yahya with the title takes one back to why the Báb wrote about Jusuf in His first Tablet, instead of directly pointing to Husayn Ali, i.e. Baha'ullah' for had anyone found out that He was to come forth after the Báb,, He would have had many difficulties, some of which would have delayed the Cause. For was not "Husayn' the Arabic numerical equivalent of "Jusuf"? Referring to the name of Mirza Yahya, Adib quotes the Blessed Beauty:

> **"Furthermore, alluding to Mirza Yahya whose title was Subh-i-Azal (Morning of Eternity), He asserts that through His power the untrue morn was completely darkened.(3)"**
>
> **(The Revelation of Bahá'u'lláh v 2, p. 2)**

Yet instead Mirza Yahya, seemed to be working to the community's destruction. Frequently in fear of his life, he traveled in disguise to Baghdad in order to rejoin the exiled Bábís, but once there cast the community into confusion and went so far as to have some of the Bábís assassinated. Bahá'u'lláh references Yahyá a number of times in His Tablets. Taken all together, the Tablets revealed during this period, *The Hidden Words*, and the *Kitáb-i-Íqán* shaped the Bábís' understanding of the new Revelation, the state of their community, and things to come while increasing their dedication and willingness to sacrifice to the Cause of the Báb. Through these Books and Tablets, and through Bahá'u'lláh's own example, they came to understand how precious their new Faith was, and emboldened them to lay down their very lives in the Path of God. At the time of being banished from Iran, Bahá'u'lláh had not yet revealed Himself as a Manifestation but was known as being prominent in the Bábi Faith. That declaration came when He was being further banished to Constantinople, at which time, in the Garden of Ridvan, while preparing to depart for Constantinople, He intimated this declaration, though it is not recounted exactly how He did that, since at that time he had proved Himself worthy beyond doubt of much and needed very little to prove any point. At that major juncture in His history He had already revealed the two notable Books mentioned above. Up to this point though, Bahá'u'lláh seemed to have only been known by the name of Jinab-i-Baha, a name acquired at the Conference at Badasht in 1848 where most believers found new names from Him. From this point on Bahá'u'lláh acquired many names and descriptions among the Bahá'ís, one of which is Bahá'u'lláh. He is addressed as the Blessed Perfection, the Ancient Beauty, the Most Glorious Beauty etc…One would have to read about the Valley of Names that Adib Taherzadeh speaks of in his *Revelation of Bahá'u'lláh Vol I.* We note that the first Book of the Báb was the Qayyum'ul Asma or Eternal Names. Those eternal names, God and His Manifestations have.

Thus transitioned the Bábi's to the Bahá'í Faith we know today. With the first books Bahá'u'lláh pointed the way of the new religion, with ample proof and testimonies, a religion which bases itself on actions rather than copious words as proof of belief. Thus religion has to improve lives of believers in the Manifestation through obedience to His command. Many are the texts which could be added here supportive of this theme in religion. The one below is chosen as being the most direct:

> **The first duty prescribed by God for His servants is the recognition of Him Who is the Day Spring of His Revelation and the Fountain of His 331 laws, Who representeth the Godhead in both the Kingdom of His Cause and the world of creation. Whoso achieveth this duty hath attained unto all good; and whoso is deprived thereof, hath gone astray, though he be the author of every righteous deed. It behoveth every one who reacheth this most sublime station, this summit of transcendent glory, to observe every ordinance of Him Who is the Desire of the world. These twin duties are inseparable. Neither is acceptable without the other. Thus hath it been decreed by Him Who is the Source of Divine inspiration.**
>
> *(Gleanings from the Writings of Bahá'u'lláh, p. 330)*

Leaders and Religion

Jesus was crucified at the request of the religious leaders of his day both secular and religious. Muhammad was persecuted by the leaders of Mecca who caused Him much harm, one of the worst being His maternal uncle Abu Lahab. The Báb was executed on the orders of the court of Tabríz after several years of imprisonment, being subjected to the bastinado, and interrogations. His worst enemies were the Ulamas (the scholars and authorities of Islam), the Mullas, and the Mujtahids (those qualified to pronounce judgments and decisions with respect to Islamic law). Likewise, religious authorities denounced Bahá'u'lláh and agitated for His banishment and imprisonment, leading to not only several months of dungeon imprisonment, but to a further imprisonment which was never revoked until He ascended, a period of forty years...

The leaders of religion have always been at the forefront of the persecution of the Manifestations of God. Proud of their knowledge and status, fearful of anything that might upset the tidy order of their worlds, they lash out at God's Messengers instead of investigating and judging fairly. Thus they have caused the Manifestations untold suffering. Their fate is bound with their opposition to God: Caiaphas and Pilate are remembered only for their roles in Jesus' crucifixion and nothing more. Again the Valley of Names and Attributes!

Bahá'u'lláh in the Kitab-i-Iqan has mentioned some Manifestations Who are not named a lot in the Bible, but remembering that even prophets in the Apocrypha are not mentioned there, it would seem there is much we do not know about all prophets revealed by God in several books. Surely eons of ages of humans have passed through this earth, and it would be a sin to accuse the Just God we have of not having revealed everything to them. Therefore, it stands to reason that there were Manifestations before our times of which we know not, and salvation of man from his own wrongdoing could not have begun in One A.D. That would mean that generations of humans had no God nor did they have guidance. To me that would be very unwise to accuse Our Creator of, for He creates what becomes of each soul and nurtures each created thing. Therefore again we must find the answers to the symbolism in the Writings we have. To do this, Bahá'ís combine search by science with search by faith and spiritual understanding. Who would for example say where I would have been, had I dreamed of a place, people and conversation, and in ten years see the place and hear that conversation? The Blessed Perfection mentions also that there were languages and peoples not known today. It does not surprise me therefore to find names like Hud and Salih mentioned elsewhere in the Qur'an as having been Prophets. One example is Salih Whom Baha'u;llah writes about and is associated with the Salih in the Genesis Book of the Bible.

10:24 And Arphaxad begat Salah; and Salah begat Eber.

(King James Bible, Genesis)

11:14 And Salah lived thirty years, and begat Eber: 11:15 And Salah lived

after he begat Eber four hundred and three years, and begat sons and daughters.

(King James Bible, Genesis)

Consider the differences that have arisen since the days of Adam. The divers and widely-known languages now spoken by the peoples of the earth were originally unknown, as were the varied rules and customs now prevailing amongst them. The people of those times spoke a language different from those now known. Diversities of language arose in a later age, in a land known as Bábel. It was given the name Bábel, because the term signifieth "the place where the confusion of tongues arose."

(Gleanings from the Writings of Bahá'u'lláh, p. 173)

It is known that the Bible was translated from two languages, Hebrew for the Old Testament, and Greek for the New Testament, the second being of course because Jesus spoke more and taught in Aramaic. It would not be surprising to find out the language spoken in those times would involve both Hebrew and Aramaic., Aramaic being an ancient language in that region of the world., and so His teaching was recorded a hundred year later as such, as valid as they are,,. and then taken to many other languages from those translations. For many years, therefore, there had to be someone who knew more about such languages and Latin which were predominant, but not today in our age. In those years then arose the priesthood and all associated with it, in assisting believers to understand the Holy Writ and interpret it for the common person who had no access. Today we realize language to be the blowing of air through the mouth to manifest what goes on in the mind. If it is a bad thought, it does not really matter how pretty we make it sound it remains bad. Actions tell.

Historically, Rome having the interconnection of routes became very important, resulting in the centralization of the Cause of Christ in Rome initially for, from there traffic could be directed to several parts of Europe and the surrounds. The phrase that " All roads lead to Rome " was true then! This was how the teaching of Christianity was organized from onset of the effort. For Emperor Constantine had recognized Christianity as a church of the state then for the first time in he history of that Cause.

> **Unable to crush Christianity by persecution, Roman emperors decided to gain the support of the growing number of Christians within the Empire. In A.D. 313 Constantine, genuinely attracted to Christianity issued the Edict of Milan granting tolerance to Christians.. By A.D. 392 Theodosius I had made Christianity the state religion of the Empire, and declared the worship of pagan gods illegal.**

> **(Perry, p.129)**

It is very true, therefore, that in past ages relatively few had sufficient education to read and comprehend the Holy Books. Today with education widely available, almost anyone can do so. We need no longer rely upon the knowledge of others to access the Books of God. We all have access to our Creator through the words of His Manifestations—Jesus, Muhammad, Krishna, the Buddha, the Báb, Bahá'u'lláh— without the need for others among our peers to interpret and codify on our behalf. Moreover, we should not let the Kingdom of Names cast us into confusion—that is, that the Manifestation of God has appeared with different names at different times should not be a cause for division, hatred or conflict. Through them, humanity has been uplifted and mighty civilizations raised. The time is past to consider any one of them superior to others.

Indeed, Bahá'u'lláh has removed authority from ecclesiastics and kings and given all responsibility for their own spiritual development. We no longer need intermediaries between us and the Manifestation of God. He is the only intermediary we need. Just as we cannot approach the sun directly but can perceive its light and warmth from a distance, the Holy Ones declare God's mystery through the power of the Holy Spirit. The Holy Spirit can be likened to the clouds from which the rain falls, causing the growth of all things. Through the Holy Spirit we receive the inspiration that underlies all human arts and science. Small wonder that They should have stressed the preciousness of the opportunities which it was in the power of these rulers and leaders to seize, and should have warned them in ominous tones of the grave responsibilities which the rejection of God's Message would entail, and should have predicted, when rebuffed and refused, the dire consequences which such a rejection involved. Small wonder that He Who is the King of Kings and Vicegerent of God Himself should, when abandoned, condemned and persecuted, have uttered this epigrammatic and momentous prophecy:

> **"From two ranks amongst men power hath been seized: kings and ecclesiastics."**
>
> **(The Promised Day is Come, p. 19)**

A Comment

When I was in a college at Fort Hare, I met a man later who became a good friend. We met in one of those school argument groups that were so common in those days. The subject was religion, and in the argument the religion of Islam was being disputed. I found out the chief arguments against favoring Islam were from a man who was Catholic. I was a new Baha'i.

I had attended school in a township high school, and the man had been to a boarding school near the college, which was Lovedale Institution. The man held sway in the argument and I decided to take him on.

We started arguing after dinner,(about 6:30 p.m.) an talked until about 2:00 a.m.. In the end, tired as I was, I won. For the man started by saying" I agree that Muhammad did the same kind of work Jesus did…" I stopped him and asked:" Why then are we arguing?" I knew he had not finished his statement but he had basically agreed with me. He tried to extend time, and I told him that it was time for bed, and lectures would soon begin. That ended the day. I congratulated myself because then I was a "fresher" at college. I had already earned a reputation of being able to argue.

The man then asked me to prove my point that all religions speak the same truth, by going to communion with him, for one morning, on a Sunday. I did, and it was at 6:00 a.m. that arose from bed to prove a point!

The man was the now deceased Dr. Sam Nolutshungu, who had left South Africa later on an " Exit Permit" never to return. Having left, I learned three years later that he was at Keele University in the United Kingdom and had earned his degree. We corresponded briefly.. His sister who was doing midwifery at the local hospital found out that I knew him. She must have been Catholic too for her name was Mary.

Later when I was in the United States, I called Sam, and found out he was then a doctor in Political Science. For reasons I did not quite understand, he left Keele and came to New York, where I again called him.

Reading a newspaper one day from South Africa, I learned that my friend had passed on, The reason for the change was that he had a problem with cancer. His return home was after independence and he had had to turn down an appointment to Chancellorship at the Witwatersrand University.

At the end of the first year, Sam and I spent a week at his home, for he invited me so we could get to know each other. I had a course to write in Geography and had an upgrade of my certificate for high school, and so had to return to the college after that week. My surprise that night, was after being invited by the Botany demonstrator to dinner, and finding out that very night that the President of the United States had been assassinated. For it was a Friday November 22[nd,] 1963. The man I was with, a Hindu, was also astounded, for he had seen me visited by an American Consul in Iona House, during the opening of the Federal Seminary in Alice, South Africa earlier in 1963. That is the very reason I am able to remember the time.

For some reason I never had much problem as a Baha' with Catholics. In my second year I had friends from Kimberley who all four were Catholic. My friend whose mother was Bahá'í,, a Radiographer, was from the United States and also Catholic.

Sam and I in the second year were co-producers of a play called:" A Night at an Inn" where he played the thug and I the boss of a couple of thugs. We had our fun, yet religiously we respected each others' ground. Two fellows from Kimberley were not happy I did not return to school the following year, and so took a train trip to visit Port Elizabeth. Perhaps it is knowing a few Catholics that persuaded me to tell a man I knew he was Catholic by his attitude, only to find that he was a Catholic priest! I amazed him and never explained as we got of an airplane together one night in Port Elizabeth…

Such relationships are precious, for 'religion" means "to bring together" hence Religion is a uniting factor among Jews and Gentiles alike. If one respects the tenets of another's religion it makes a difference in getting on together. Heaven is known to none, for none has ever returned to tell us how to get there except the Manifestations,Whom we always deny and give a hard time in teaching their Faith.

Having substantiated knowing Sam Nolutshungu, I can now show a snapshot of his life:

I met "Sam" Nolutshungu in 1963 in Alice, South Africa, at the Fort Hare University College where he studied for a diploma as a teacher. He was a student from Lovedale Boarding School. When he was student at the college, he was allowed at graduations to give a short talk on behalf of the students. Later Sam, a very active member of the student body, had to leave the country for the United Kingdom because of the political atmosphere. He wrote me a note once with an address at Keele University in the United Kingdom, but was quiet for some years. Before he left, he had invited me to his home in Fort Beaufort to spend a week with him. In 1969 I met his cousin named Mary, who w as studying for a Nursing Certificate in Port Elizabeth who informed me that Sam had graduated in a B.A. at Keele University.

When I moved to the United States in 1987, I researched Keele University and found a telephone number. I called to find out to my surprise that Sam had then attained a PhD in Political Science. We exchanged telephone conversations for a while before I was told that he had moved to New York in the United States. Later Sam moved to South Africa after that country attained independence for the Black population. There was no method by which I could then speak to him again, but on reading newspapers from South Africa I learned that he had turned down appointment to Chancellorship at a university in South Africa. Sam did that because he was unwell. I soon read in the newspapers that he passed on in South Africa. When I learned that I then understood why he had moved around that much.

Resurrection

In certain Holy Books and traditions, a promise is given of resurrection and final judgment. In the end, they say, people will be raised up from the dead, judged, and given reward or punishment as it is due. Many people believe this will happen physically and even that the Earth itself will be destroyed and remade as an eternal home for the righteous or that this event will signal the end the existence of the universe.

But there are problems with this literal view of resurrection. For one thing, the sheer number of people who have lived since the dawn of humanity is said to be about one hundred and eight billion according to some authorities, as opposed to the seven billion who currently inhabit the Earth at the present time. However, even there one has to take account of all births and deaths in that time, an event which alters the total rapidly. That would make for quite a crowd, especially if most of us are redeemable! Even if only a paltry one-quarter of us were redeemable (that is, if the supposedly merciful God sends three quarters of us to eternal damnation), the Earth would still be overtaxed. And that doesn't even take into consideration that the lucky few might get to have children.

For another, we have to consider that preceding generations are not dissimilar to us. In each generation there are some who are very good, some who are very bad, and a great many who fall into the broad area in between. God is just but also merciful. He would not excessively punish our wrongdoing, and He offers us forgiveness if we turn to Him. The number of religions that have existed throughout time testify to the many times He has reached out His merciful hands to us. So it seems far more likely that most of those one hundred and eight billion people can have some sort of path to reunion with Him and can, one way or another, obtain a share of paradise. It is not said when this event will occur, or if at all it has ever repeated itself like an astronomical occurrence. In a way, this would entail a one time sucking up of all existence. Is this possible? Considering that the Lord wrought up creation from nothing, only to return it to nothing with no special intervening event to justify the creation logically. This itself would show the futility of the creation itself. Yet there seems reason and logic in existence, that we can discern in the laws attending that existence. Why the sudden end with no reasoning attending it?

So what is resurrection, then? Is it the physical recreation of a body long since decayed? Or is it a spiritual reality? An awakening from the sleep of negligence to the wakefulness of knowledge? A revival of Faith in God in a heart darkened by attachment to lesser things? A transformation from selfishness and greed to selflessness and charity?

Is it not, in fact, a renewal of all that existed or known, philosophically, spiritually, socially and otherwise into a new understanding and consciousness of itself? Is it not the rejuvenation of our manners and understanding of the reality of our world and all that this entails? This sort of resurrection is dramatic and logical, because were we to consider the apples of one year we would find them manifest in the next with any difference at all except time. The deeds of spiritual valor would again persist and be discerned in any present time or circumstance. This itself lays the burden of recognizing a spiritual springtime upon each individual.

Just as one cannot have a blanket peace, but an agreed upon situation, this event follows also logically. We would settle down to another period of some peace and tranquil existence until something we do not quite understand makes its presence known. The redefinition of reality must persist as it has done before. In our time it encompasses not just time, but the attending events. No longer is heaven in the sky but we are challenged by having to visit our Moon. We look to space and ask:" Can we get there?" or " Are we permitted?". The answer would be "Why not?" We say " I think, therefore I am". The thinking is the function of our existence, and imagination gets us to areas we never knew before. Why stint that, when our Creator talks of Eternity?

The coming of the apples of divine spring time, is the renewal of civilization and the coming of new laws, the coming of a new and present Manifestation of the Deity and His Eternity. A reminder that we progress, this world and the next. The saying is:"He neither sleeps or wakes, the God of Israel". This thing was given to us in the very analogy of the party for the rich Jesus talks of which resulted in all of us being brought in.. Our awakening to Him is not also His awakening to us, if he has eternally existed, with or without us. We the mere image we have to strive towards manifesting!

In each era our understanding of Him is renewed. The laws applying to each age are altered and extended. The bringing together in the word 'religion' testifies to His existence as One Indivisible Creator and a Creator creates! Each time we have to know what to do and what is expected of us in pleasing Him and attaining our progress in all the worlds He has.

It is obvious that as we die we stand before Him to account for all deeds anyway, this being to me, an assessment of where we seem to be in development that gives survival in the next stage, the mere analogy of growing wings with no air around!. This is itself advancing into worlds we are prepared for in this existence. Just as a chicken knows little about the egg and still has to come out of it, we are growing and preparing for that appearance, and we dare not stint ourselves of all those tools we shall need in that world by not picking them up in this world of existence. For therein lies our progress. Why would we have birds developing wings in an egg? We have to learn from thee very little things, always remembering the analogy of the ant we have to go to for wisdom!

When the gown known as religion is worn, it is renewed by none other but Himself, for He knows best the way we are to go from stage to stage of the unfolding of our reality?

The Veil of Knowledge

We are always learning. The day we stop learning is the day we die, in reality, a situation well nigh impossible to attain as we are naturally that way. Reality of knowledge is not a figment of the mind. Knowledge is acclaimed in the Holy Writings as one of the attributes of God, and its acquisition is not merely praised but enjoined upon us. Nevertheless, it is said that knowledge is the most grievous veil separating man from God. Why should this be? What we sometimes claim to know gives us a feeling of wellbeing that we do not after all need God. We feel we know reality as should be known, a situation which is always false in its premise. If we knew the very foundations of reality we could claim to know, but who knows that, knowledge being all that is knowable? We even feel we know the foundations and realities of creation without ever establishing just in whose area the universe grows or attains existence in. If random, why the laws of discovery? If not, what actuates it to an existence? If it actuated itself, how does it attain a reality of knowing itself without an existence in the first place.? These questions boggle the mind and yet there are those who claim they know the answers, and cannot account for either their dreams that come true nor the very existence itself in which they are involved, and need a death in the end. We could go *ad infinitum* in this vein without attaining an end!

In one saying knowledge is defined to be twenty seven letters and that all that we have attained as two letters of that and that we need to attain the remaining twenty five. It is clear that the alphabet of many nations does have twenty seven letters and that all we can express can be expressed in those letters. Not all we express is even known. Even Evolution with all evidence is still in question to many. Genealogy becomes a great problem as we consider ourselves smaller or greater than others in existence. Can we prove this? It seems daunting to prove entirely, but we can prove a common origin.

When they come with knowledge not manifest in our books, limited as they are, we refute them and call them many unsavory names.

It is true that a learned man may find difficulty in learning from a manifestly unlearned one, but what is our knowledge? Galileo suffered at the hands of those of religion for trying to prove scientific law (Durant W..and A.) What do we learn from this?

There are two types of knowledge we have. One is superstitious and the other is reality. Superstition is belief in something that cannot be proven by fact. There are many such beliefs we cling to without any reason to do so, except fear of loss of superiority or being ousted in what we think we know. When God sends one as a teacher, and He mentions things we know nothing about, we call Him a liar, and later acclaim Him great. Caiaphas and Pilate might have gained from Jesus had they inquired, but Mary and Peter who were not qualified in anything but belief and faith took the title of belief in Jesus. What then is knowledge? The thief crucified with Jesus testified to His Holiness and was promised an immediate meeting in the next world without any delay. Knowing the truth is a qualification of supremacy in knowledge, and this in itself humbles one, for one comes to know that one has not even scratched the surface of knowledge. It is very difficult for one accustomed to teaching others with authority to take up the part of student.

Generalizations are spurious statements not accompanied by any proof in support and soon become a nuisance. To prove belief one must practice belief. To tell of how others did it is no proof that one desires the same way. I therefore have to believe in facts and proven thoughts in establishing a stand. It is fact that no one has died and returned to tell of it, so no one is an authority in that matter. I have to establish a lifesyle of my own and by myself, by observing, listening and practicing. Any other way would be too difficult for me to negotiate. I can tell my thoughts on the matter but this is no reason anyone should believe me without digesting them just because I, a humble believer, trying to attain His good-pleasure should be taken as being true..

A stone is a stone, is a stone! I can use that as an analogy that when one does not comprehend, one may be likened to a stone which is static and not dynamic. This dynamic stance applies to humans in that the human attains knowledge and can upgrade it. The human has to realize that what is discovered may not be final. The mind of man needs to be finite for as the religion attests it is a creation. Can it then know the very Creator as He knows Himself? I may create a robot, but is doubtful if it will ever comprehend me for I function, not only on logic but on wisdom and virtue. What seems logical to do may be dangerous in effect. It can endanger other considerations that I have to take into account, in any decision I make. Origins of what we discover may be easier to handle, however, if the source from which the first knowledge was attained was proven for all time as trustworthy. Such evidence thus needs be trusted to attain a state of a truism.

A phenomenon observed does not have to be based on superstition, but may needs confirmatory observations of occurrence to establish its ruling and law. Thus we can employ it to serve humankind. To dismiss all as mere superstition while observing the occurrence regularly happening would be very foolish indeed!

One kind of knowledge emanates from the divine, and another from limited minds who profess to know. Thus one is divine and the other satanic, not that anyone invisible has anything to do with it, but because an evil mind designs it and proves it in a limited way, and in seeking recognition advances it as truth disdaining all proof from the wise or the contrary.. In olden day the belief was that heaven is in the sky, today,, we have just landed on the Moon. Height as such are debunked, for the height we must attain is not that height. It is spiritual but a manifest reality in that it is palpable if one knows any spirituality at all. This has nothing to do with magic, but can be associated in a way with other phenomena occurring in our world and, such as are relegated to being either mystical or mythical. What if a man heals by holding hands and it works; what if he tells events that actually occur etc. there are many examples which point to this that we do not really know ourselves. In my religion, activities of that nature, named as psychic, are not to be deliberately activated as they belong to a world we have to attain later, but are known to be there. All our mind can comprehend is that which can be explained in twenty seven letters and no more. In the fullness of time that is promised as an ability we can aspire to, and that is knowing all the letters of knowledge, and at this time we do not comprehend to the extent that we should. Mere images of the Reality are we… A reflection of thoughts expressed may need be considered coming from one crying for a need to understand…the very coming of Manifestations of the Virtues of God to humans.

Knowing God is hard to come by, and knowing Him forces one to obey Him. Carl Yung(Jung, p. 45-47) in one book names this encounter as a defining moment in experiencing God, and that one never forgets it. Many Manifestations tell of a one time experience which defines all Their lives. One has to go through it to know it, and cannot depend on hearsay. However, knowing about Him may lead one to knowing Him. That seems like rhetoric but is very true and there is no other way of expressing it. Shakespeare mentions words to the effect that knowing my deed is more like not knowing myself, but knowing one's self truly can be tantamount to knowing God. But who knows one's true self? Very few...if any, outside the Manifestations. Striving after the knowledge of God needs to be accompanied by deeds of faith, so that one gains assistance about many things one never thought one would ever know, for they may be hidden from eyes for long a time.

Many people regard this stance of deeds as being spurious, but then does the human really know where he is to result in ending up this life or any other? All is theory and doubt. The sure knowledge has to come from one who has been tested, and who then disdains and abandons this life and gives it, so that others would,learn and get to know what is desired by the Supreme Ruler of them while they are in His creation.

I then end with these words on this theme, that to search for God is to search for one's true self and know that thoroughly. " He knows God, who knows himself"

> **In this connection, He Who is the eternal King -- may the souls of all that dwell within the mystic Tabernacle be a sacrifice unto Him -- hath spoken: "He hath known God who hath known himself."**
>
> **(Gleanings from the Writings of Bahá'u'lláh, p. 178)**

A Thought on reality

We say "The sky is the limit" at one time, only to realize that this is not the limit. Again we say: "reach for the stars", only to find that no man can do that. We say we see, only to realize that what we say we see is a stack of atoms perceived by eyes that are made of atoms. What then is reality? Across cultures what we behold is interpreted differently depending on the culture. So social norms are not a determinant of reality. We execute an action and it appears to be good or bad. The fact is that it not the action that is so important but what actuates it, the values we hold to. The values themselves are what we learn of good and bad. Good and bad are derived from a religious system. That brings about the thought that religious truth is itself progressive and not static. What appears to be wrong according to religion may appear to be right in subsequent years of religion. There is determining how the real, the value system applies. An action can be accidentally right or accidentally wrong depending on how the action is perceived by society, but this does not change the intention of the action So the determinant of the origins of the action within the self is important. Was it for ill for or for good, and what ill and good according to the person are. Again 'according 'to the person. This is because we come from various backgrounds. If we had a universal background we would have a universal value system, and therefore a more or less knowable good and bad.

Seen in this argument above, the self in determining good and bad is involved and tied up to the action it executes. This shifts the balance because there is no good or bad unless we have a determinant of good and bad. Yet good and bad change in each era. What we see with our eyes is known only to itself, how we perceive of it may vary. What is reality then but the thing itself, whatever it is, and it is known only to itself. We cannot and must have a statement of' "my truth and your truth", for that would mean that the thing we see is determined by what each person knows of it and not of itself. The truth stays that "It is what it is".

What we know as good and bad is therefore related to time and circumstance. That is the reason that even religious truth is dependent on time and circumstance. How do we find some value that is not determined by time? For that we do not look to what we term the 'tangible' but resort to the 'intangible". Social norms vary from continent to continent and from time to time. Can we alter love and mercy? Those remain in any culture but are expressed in various ways. The most important thing therefore in determining right and wrong is the value system associated, not with norms, but ethics, where ethics stands for moral a values sometimes referred to as virtues.

In this issue virtues are attributes which determine one's values of actions. These originate from some system we term religion. No culture can do without those. Love, knowledge, understanding, mercy, grace are among them. They are not measurable or quantifiable, but each individual has to learn to live up to them. One assumes that the very end o and extreme of all of them would be the very qualities of whatever made the essence of the human. People have called that God. If we apply the principle of " for every good there is a greater good" we might find that the greatest good is what made the good in the first place. One would then say that that is not easy to comprehend but no one ever said the mind of the human can comprehend " all things". He discovers that as he goes along without altering his innate value system that he carries with him,,that value system being intangible in nature.

Reality therefore can only be what we see as not shifting with time or circumstance. The universe itself may shift with time: is it intangible, yes it is material, and exists as a material entity we know not. For without its existence, what would be there but what caused it to appear?

The world of man is bounded by time, and everything in it shifts with time. All understanding makes sense in terms of time. At one time a thing is allowable according to a Book, at another it is tabooed. The only common threads are those things which caused cohesion among beings, the associations of togetherness and actions affecting beings as a whole in any society, and at any time.

This brings up again the notion of why values should be universal in our world. A common value system has to be known for a common good to apply. A good is only learned and never born with any individual. The only ones who take up good are individuals who appear from time to humans to state and restate good and bad. Often we kill these, for the somewhat upset the balance of how we exist. Until the new good and bad is learned and the upset will become a calm.

Reality of what we are is not in the atoms that form us, but in the conception of what we are, if that itself does not seem go in a circle. We do not really know what we are. To look objectively at each person is not enough for actions are determined from within. Therefore, the mine of knowledge of man is within. We can perceive nature and all things through atomic eyes, but we really perceive each himself with no eyes but a truer knowledge. It is then the self that has to know itself deeply, so that it knows the others. Knowing the self is knowing the originator.

Physically man is a combination of the mineral, plant, animal and human worlds. Therefore going down to the roots of who we are as individually is in fact going down to knowing this world. Knowing oneself is then the reality. Knowing any other is superficial, but truly knowing the self is not, if viewed with a mind that does not try to bias itself, and takes on a dispassionate view of life.

The phrase then that we sometimes hear of that " He has known God who knows himself" has to be true. Sometimes what we think we are is different from what we really are. Therefore it is not just the thinking of what we think we are, but the real thinking of where we stand as humans with regard to what is regarded as ideal behavior, ideal behavior itself determined by some universal book society knows about. We in society decided to exist together, and we in society decided to adhere to a set of behaviors that determine us. What if that behavior involves every being and in every society? Would that not create a reality of one world?

We see ourselves as being alone in a vast universe but how we determine the loneliness is determined by ourselves tied to the planet and never having been anywhere else. Can it really be true? The truth is that what we do, make the statement in what we call the "real world" which itself is determined by a world which is invisible in our minds. The mind itself is the creative machine which originates and the great mind determine what the rest will come to know as reality. Such that reality, just as religious truth, changes with time. But does not alter the system that determines our true values, the virtues. They, the virtues, are the basis of judging any action trough time, which makes it easy to say that we can be judged on our actions determined by those unchanging values at any time in any era.

The question becomes: What are our value systems today, when technology has so advanced.? In fact, how do we apply our innate virtues to an altered society? With the change in what is known, that application has also to change. It is no longer a case of the country of origin that is at stake, but the origin of being an Earthling, aspiring to go into a broader universal area of existence, which requires a universal norm, or set of behavioral values.

The fact it that, we cannot grasp the nature of reality for our era until we grasp our nature of ourselves for the time and era. Changes of discovery have altered and we have to alter our stance of what we think we are. We can start by applying the seem values in an altered way that suits the time, and that itself desires a mind to point the way. I would then imagine that whatever that way has to be it has to define itself as universal, a reason why I took up being a Bahá'i which is not just a religious system but a way of life.

Obscuring Clouds

When I was a young man, the verse from the Gospel, **"And then shall they see the Son of man coming in the clouds with great power and glory"** (Mk 13:26, KJV; also see Mk 14:62; Mt 24:30, 26:64; Lk 21:27)…. confused me. Did it mean that Jesus would float down from a cloudy sky?

Or did it refer to the manner of his dress? Perhaps He would be clothed in white robes in the likeness of clouds?

Eventually I found my answer in the Holy Writings of the Bahá'í Faith. Bahá'u'lláh explains that these clouds signify whatever makes it difficult for us to recognize Him: He would be born into the world as a child; like us, he would eat and sleep and perhaps fall ill; he might marry and have a family. Through death he would pass out of this world again. In other words, outwardly he would appear very much a human being. As a result, we might ask, "How can this be Christ returned? He is nothing that we expected!"

In one of His Books Bahá'u'lláh has written that God could utter one letter and cause all to become believers, but such is not His plan. He wishes us to seek and find Him of our own free will. To that end He has given us the faculties necessary to seek and find: the potent combination of heart and mind. He stands ready to assist, and His bounties surround us always, but we must want His assistance. **"If thou lovest Me not, my love can in no wise reach thee."** (*The Hidden Words*, Arabic 5.) Once we take the step of search, His love is there to help us along the way. We may then discover that He reveals Himself in the simplest of ways, each and every day. Through prayer and deeds, we find the doors of knowledge of God opened wide.

Thus the search for God is both spiritual and scientific: spiritual because it requires devotion and purity, scientific because it requires making use of the mind. Although we might wish for some clear sign, some miracle that will reveal God's presence and make everything clear in a moment, that is not God's way. It has been noted that in the Gospels, Jesus never performs a miracle to prove Himself. He performs miracles to help others, and specifically to help those who have already professed their belief in Him and sought His help. The same is true of the Báb and Bahá'u'lláh. To those who denied them and demanded wonders before they would believe, they basically said, "No."

In addition to the "clouds" pertaining to the Manifestation of God Himself, there are others. People often judge a religion by its followers rather than by its teachings. While this is understandable, it can lead us astray. None of us is perfect, after all, and within any religion there are people of widely varying spiritual development. Some may be very spiritual, while others may be quite the opposite. People often pay more attention to the bad examples than the good ones. But to reject the Manifestation of God on that account is far from rational.

Clouds, then, are those things which intervene between us and the recognition of God's Messenger. Today God calls us to unity, yet how divided we are! He has indeed "come in the clouds" and those clouds have kept many of us from recognizing Him. All of His sufferings are bound up in this.

The meaning of healing in the Message of the Christ takes on new meaning when one views it from the angle of spirituality. Take for an example the idea of my neighbor. It is known that Samaritans were shunned by all Jews because they mixed families with Armenians while the Jews were in captivity in Bábylon or present day Iran. However, Jesus makes the Samaritan a neighbor and a helpful one at that. The example of healing of Lazarus tells us how we can be dead spiritually in belief and be revived in faith by God Himself through calling us from the sepulcher of self into life of the spirit. If Jesus were to heal a lame man and another lame child should be born the next day, how is that to be viewed as a long lasting cure? But is we think of all the spiritually lame persons in the world and how they could be healed we realize that we heal them for this life and the next. These are just a few ways of looking at healing and seeing that the healing spiritually is more of primal importance than a physical healing. Besides, how are those who did not see the healing to believe? Can we prove this? But if we show how a nonbeliever becomes true to God through the words of spirituality then there is a manifest gain!

The fruits of a Prophet or Manifestation are the rules He presents for the preservation of life and nations. Thus Jesus speaks of the fruit of the Manifestation as being the laws He will present. Can they preserve life? Can they serve the purposes of the protection of humankind for ages to come? The answer will then spell the belief…

Rising from the dead

There is widespread belief that at the end of time all who have ever lived will be restored to life and judged. As mentioned before, this seems paradoxical, since the number of people who must be brought back to life is so large that the Earth could not contain them all. Moreover, God has placed us in an orderly universe that obeys certain laws. Such events as are often attributed as occurences of the "end times" defy all order and logic. Why would God create a universe that appears to function in a certain way, only to throw all into confusion at some predetermined moment? What would have been the purpose of that creation then?

I used to find it difficult to accept that my ancestors,

who had beliefs different from mine, would at some point be judged without having had the benefit of knowing Christ. How could the generations before His advent or before the spread of the Gospel be condemned for not being Christian? They had religions that guided their lives, even though it was not Christianity and even though the details of their beliefs may have differed considerably from my own. Surely if they tried to follow those beliefs, that is what mattered most!

Later, I came to understand resurrection in a different light: a spiritual one rather than a physical one. Let us revisit the thief crucified on Calvary, as he offers a clear example of this issue. Luke writes:

> **And one of the malefactors which were hanged railed on him, saying, If thou be Christ, save thyself and us.**
>
> **But the other answering rebuked him, saying, Dost not thou fear God, seeing thou art in the same condemnation? And we indeed justly; for we receive the due reward of our deeds: but this man hath done nothing amiss.**
>
> **And he said unto Jesus, Lord, remember me when thou comest into thy kingdom.**
>
> **And Jesus said unto him, Verily I say unto thee, To day shalt thou be with me in paradise.**
>
> (Luke 23:39-43, KJV)

This is a striking case of spiritual resurrection at the hour of physical death! Here is a thief, one who has lived his life in wickedness, recognizing Jesus, professing faith in Him, and asking to be remembered by Him. And Jesus responds with assurance that, on that very day the thief would be in paradise. He has been transformed in a moment, not physically but spiritually, raised to new spiritual life.

This spiritual awakening is what Bahá'u'lláh refers to when he uses the metaphor of copper changed to gold, cited previously. Many nonbelievers have been similarly transformed, spiritually rising from death. In this context, 'Abdu'l-Bahá remarked, "Unless we perceive reality, we cannot understand the meanings of the Holy Books, for these meanings are symbolical and spiritual -- such as, for instance, the raising of Lazarus, which has spiritual interpretation." (*The Promulgation of Universal Peace*, p. 245, ¶ 87.3)

Another form of resurrection might be the general rejuvenation of the fortunes of humankind through the coming of the Manifestation of God. Before His advent, the world is as dead. Before He proclaims Himself and begins to teach, we are like people wandering lost in the woods. But once He is among us, He creates a new culture and a new world, resurrecting a dead society.

Bahá'u'lláh also makes the example of the days of the week or the risings and settings of the sun. Except for what we do per day, all he days are the same rising and setting of the sun. In that sense all rejuvenation of humankind through a new day is the same, except for the requirements of that time.

In a similar way, the apples of one year are the same as

those of the next. No one will refuse apples because they are of a new season. Were we to do that, survival would have been unthinkable. So we accept the Law of God as it comes after determining that first it fulfills prophecy, second the Person is not working towards any remuneration, thirdly that what He says is logical and healthy physically and spiritually. With those thoughts in place, realization of the bread of life which comes at each season from God becomes a possibility and a concrete matter, for those would rejuvenate the fortunes of humankind, the laws of existence would apply aptly. If, as Bahá'u'lláh states, copper is chemically changed to gold, no one can claim that, that gold is copper. So then, when one acknowledges belief in the Manifestation of God, that one changes completely, so completely as to be unrecognizable compared to the original seeker after God. For in some way, we all are seekers after truth

Curbing our desires

A garden left to itself is soon given over to weeds, while in a well-tended garden plants are selected and arranged for their beauty or utility. We are much the same. Left to ourselves, we become self-centered and careless of the needs and feelings of others, while properly educated and trained, we develop spiritual perfections and become a blessing to those around us. These spiritual perfections—love, honesty, justice, charity, and the like—are not quantifiable, yet they are essential to our happiness and well-being. Not only that, in their perfection in the absolute sense, they would then be for the Greatest Good, or describe the Deity Himself. We are unable as humans to even visualize that. Yet, for the greater part all virtues are related one to the other.. If one perfects one virtue, one finds the others. Each leads to the other in symphony and rhythm.

What then are good and evil? Are they absolutes, or are they relative to the situation? Are they dependent upon intent, and if so how can we know the intent of another? Good intentions sometimes result in evil; can evil intent sometimes have a good outcome?

A blind man may find a door he has never before gone through by accident, but the door would be far easier to find if he could see it. Spiritually speaking, the Manifestations of God come to give sight to our blind eyes, enabling us to see the door leading to God and to pass through it. Their laws, when followed, help us recognize good and evil, in other words, and set us on the right course. It is however impossible to receive the help of God if we do not turn to Him and His laws with good intent o and obedience. For, in obedience to Him, lies the ease to His assistance and without His assistance no soul can gain admittance to Him. However, as Hooper Dunbar once remarked " God cannot guide a car if it is not moving", in other words for the guidance to reach us we should be assiduously involved in actions of obedience. Further we find another amusing remark by Ali Nakhjavani when he says that one cannot say " God take my Hand!" when one's hand is in the pocket. The second example and intent are clear and need no explanation.. This then means that our desires have to be aligned with His desire for us, to gain that assistance with better ease, though His assistance showers upon us at all times, we have to be ready and seeking to attain it for better effect.. In the song with words: " I will make you fishers of men if you follow me", this becomes more visible spiritually, for the 'if' defines the assistance. A good intent preceding a deed, even when the deed does not amount to much or ends up being negative to the intended cause, because it was honorable, becomes a benefit to the one executing it, for the heart and intent to do good were vey present. It should never be lost sight of that God can see all intent and observes all hearts. In the Bible it is said in words to the effect:"I cannot forget you, I have written you on the palm of my hand "... Therefore, for every action one intends to execute, one should measure just how far or how near that action is to His law. That to me is the determination of good and bad. In most instances, what and how people view an action that is observed as good or evil is in no way how God would view that action,, for to my limited thinking it would have to be near or far from His desire or His Law expressed in the Holy Writ to be determined either way, good or evil.. A man may die for a cause people may regard as evil, but only God knows what the intent of the one executing the act would have been, whether it was to do good or bad. Of course one has to admit that if the reason for such action was to do harm, that would be punishable. In the sense given above we cannot be judges to the actions of others whichever way one looks at the case, for we never truly know the intent of any action.. At most our justice has to do with 'harm or no harm' and not the intent of the heart. That justice has also to take place, for there is no access to the other absolute justice, except possible conjecture,and measurement of the deed. Hence in he Bible it is said" Judge not that thou mayest not be judged, for with the judgment you judge so shall ye be judged"..

7:1 Judge not, that ye be not judged.
7:2 For with what judgment ye judge, ye shall be judged: and with what measure ye mete, it shall be measured to you again.

(King James Bible, Matthew)

One never really stops being a sinner and Bahá'u'lláh says in encapsulating this state:

: 27. O SON OF MAN!

Breathe not the sins of others so long as thou art thyself a sinner. Shouldst thou transgress this command, accursed wouldst thou be, and to this I bear witness.

(Bahá'u'lláh, The Arabic Hidden Words)
There are myriads of related statements in the Holy Writ.

Death and Living

We all must die sooner or later, just as we arrive, must we also leave. The self realization that we exist must sometime reach us and we find ourselves musing about what this is all about and why, in fact, we exist. Many times in the Writings it is mentioned that this life is part of a journey to being ourselves as images of the Creator. It is therefore a very important stage. Depending on where we are when we leave, we shall either find joy or unhappiness, because there is no way of correcting living our lives and correcting all faults once we leave. Life in the worlds of God will no doubt, depend on life we live now. Outside of that, we may depend on complete mercy from the Lord. The fear that I have is that He may want to exact a penalty for all wrongs because, coming to the basis of the mercy, rather would I have that mercy than His justice, for I know just how wrong I have been on many issues of life. It is fact that in the General Systems Theory that when a system dies it manifests itself elsewhere. In support of this it is stated that a "macrocosm" has the features of a "microcosm", and that the universe has systems that are manifest in essence in each minor part. (Skyttner, 51) In essence, the forces in the universe can be manifest in an atom. Baha'uu'llah states in one tablet as quoted from poetry:

> **Split the atom's heart, and lo!**
> **Within it thou wilt find a sun. [1]**
> **[1 Persian mystic poem.]**

(The Seven Valleys, p. 12)

And again commenting on the manifestation of Muhammad, He affirms:

> **"But for Thee, I would not have**
> **created the spheres"**

(The Kitab-i-Iqan, p. 185)

To even take the statements of Bahá'u'lláh as being valid, one would have to establish first the truism of His manifestation to man, and then, after proof is established accept the Holy Writ. Accepting without the proof would not be the attitude of the Bahá'ís.Each Bahá'í has to search for the truth and declare faith in the truth on their own. This does not mean that on the very onset a Bahá'í will kow all there is to know about being a Bahai in a brief moment. But it does mean that the quest for truth for that person will have been satisfied. The analogy that suits this case is that of a man seeking water, and reaching a fountain. From that fountain that man can only drink to satisfy the thirst. It does not mean that the man will drink all the water they can get from the fountain or seek all in the reservoir of water. A Bahá'í has to be satisfied in their quest and the other things they can learn will follow in due course. In the mean time they may have to accept some of the truths as they are gradually explained.. In life, therefore we seek the truth before we seek satisfaction with earthly comforts to excess. Hence Christ makes the distinction here:

12:31 But rather seek ye the kingdom of God; and all these things shall be added unto you.

(King James Bible, Luke)

It is an analogy close tone having a penny and being willing to wait for the pennies to accumulate to ponds. One has to have a vista of a future that is prolonged and positive. Investigating the truth for any Bahá'í is a life long endeavor, for the Truth is to reach being the true image of the Deity which none on earth is, and which remains incomplete even at death. For Bahá'ís believe they develop in the worlds of God which are beyond this life on the journey to perfection to being that image. Each stage is as important as the growth of the child from babyhood to adulthood. No stage must be missed. Failure to develop is a concern for one may not know how to proceed where the guidance of the believer is no longer the earthly guidance that he missed to know while living that earthly life. This I perceive as the torment. Bahá'ís believe that progress in the worlds of God is only through His mercy and determination..In the earthly life, that progress is through the efforts of the believer and the assistance of God.

> **The soul does not evolve from degree to degree as a law -- it only evolves nearer to God, by the Mercy and Bounty of God.**
>
> (Abdu'l-Baha, Paris Talks, p. 66)

LXXXII.

Thou hast asked Me concerning the nature of the soul. Know, verily, that the soul is a sign of God, a heavenly gem whose reality the most learned of men hath failed to grasp, and whose mystery no mind, however acute, can ever hope to unravel. It is the first among all created things to declare the excellence of its Creator, the first to recognize His

> **glory, to cleave to His truth, and to bow down in adoration before Him. If it be faithful to God, it will reflect His light, and will, eventually, return unto Him. If it fail, however, in its allegiance to its Creator, it will become a victim to self and passion, and will, in the end, sink in their depths.**
>
> (Gleanings from the Writings of Baha'u'llah, p. 158)

Belief then has to be an individual action and not in concert. The undeniable fact is that, just as we are n born we are fated to die.

The reading of Skyttner's book from above pages gives one the impressions stated below. These idea were impressed upon myself as I took classes in Information Technology that without an understanding thereof I would not be a whole human sitting in front of the screen and of a computer as was the prerequisite of the study. How my own ideologies were debunked stands as a sad witness that I passed the degree " Cum Laude". How could I, I ask myself…. These were new thoughts I was assimilating! Belief and morals I could take in easily from childhood, but belief and Astronomy was new…Regardless of the fact that I often wondered as a youth what it would be like to fall off the planet!

For an example a Super Nova is said to explode but where the parts land it again creates an environment to planets and suns. We also know that, to a certain extent even atoms 'remember". Ask any Scientist he may attest this. I have of a necessity to acclaim this through study only. But we know very well that matter never is destroyed but can change from state to state. Why should this not be true for the human? What does make him or her so special that he or she can live above this law of the nature of things when he himself insists that most of what he or she is animal?

Life seems to be the mere distance between the birth and the death of a human, but what happens in between is crucial to further development, according to Bahá'u'lláh. We cannot therefore live a life of careless wanton actions when we do not really know what life to a humans should mean exactly. We accumulate experiences, but do they just vanish at death? We cannot even account for a simple thing like dreams we have and which ten years aletr manifests itself as a reality. Where then was I to see the future in the present an in my sleep. To disregard this experience would be to ignore a crucial phenomenon which needs some investigation as men and women of reason and science would do.

In this vein Baha'ullah has revealed in His Writings that:

True loss is for him whose days have been spent in utter ignorance of his self.

(Tablets of Bahá'u'lláh, p. 156)

In a world that prides itself on generations succeeding generations it is then a shame for an older person to pass this world without ever being able to impart any strategies for any future for progeny, simply because one never considered life serious enough to warrant remembering. One would query the words " serious enough ". Existence has to be a serious event, for in it holds the future of a race and that race being the human. Progress depends on what we learn now. In that sense we do not just live for ourselves but for a future. Hence a person can sacrifice a lot for the progress of others and be found worthy. Traces of our earthly existence may vanish an a century or two, but those experiences grow forever, ever drawing us nearer to the conceived picture of our being an mirror image of something greater than ourselves, which has brought this world into existence as directed by a Hand we know not. We cannot deny that we exist; the question is Why? Even Scientists know the how but not the why of things.

Daily, Bahá'ís make this affirmation. One may take this as their view and meditate on why they do take it to be so. This is prayer, they say daily:

CLXXXI

I bear witness, O my God, that Thou hast created me to know Thee and to worship Thee. I testify, at this moment, to my powerlessness and to Thy might, to my poverty and to Thy wealth.

There is none other God but Thee, the Help in Peril, the Self-Subsisting.

[Short obligatory prayer, to be recited once in twenty-four hours, at noon.]

(Prayers and Meditations by Bahá'u'lláh, p. 313)

And the following words are in many parts of the text in one form or another:

"I came forth from God, and return unto Him, detached from all save Him, holding fast to His Name, the Merciful, the Compassionate."

(, The Kitab-i-Aqdas, p. 65)

When this is considered the words of the Báb then become manifest as an issue to bring to the forefront, that at some age one should render thanks for existence:

On no account is this acceptable, inasmuch as it behooveth man, upon reaching the age of nineteen, to render thanksgiving for the day of his conception as an embryo. For had the embryo not existed, how could he have reached his present state? Likewise had the religion taught by Adam not existed, this Faith would not have attained its present stage. Thus consider thou the development of God's Faith until the end that hath no end. V, 4.

(Selections from the Writings of the Báb, p. 89)

These words give one a growing impression that it is serious issue for one who has existed not to know what one has actually done with the years one has been given to be on the planet. Even as the Christ says that a tree with no fruit is fit for the fire and no more.

> **3:10 And now also the axe is laid unto the root of the trees: therefore every tree which bringeth not forth good fruit is hewn down, and cast into the fire.**

(King James Bible, Matthew)

If we are all supposed to live the life of angels we would all not be in the realm of the human. There are, of course, those whose life is angelic but they also take the form of the human. We are to strive with heart and soul in attempting to obey, without forgetting that we are humans and have to act within that realm of being human. God understands the human aspects of our lives, He made them and imparted to them or conferred them to us to live by or with. This is an intended aim towards growth to a perfection. Thus, the humans gain a door they have to pass through. Bahá'u'lláh does ask us to act from the heart and to be true to ourselves. The matter makes this clearer in a prayer:

> **O Thou Provider! Assist Thou these noble friends to win Thy good pleasure, and make them well-wishers of stranger and friend alike. Bring them into the world that abideth forever; grant them a portion of heavenly grace; cause them to be true Bahá'ís, sincerely of God; save**

them from outward semblances, and establish them firmly in the truth.

(Selections from the Writings of
Abdu'l-Baha, p. 75)

The inner meaning seems to be of the essence, not what we appear to be but what we actually are.

It should be clear from the foregoing that religion is an assertion of the existence of a Deity, and not as is sometimes called, a method of the less privileged to legitimize their existence. Religion asserts the bringing together or all people and that they worship One Deity Who is recognized as the Supreme Authority, remaining Single and Untrammeled above all there is. Religion does not excuse itself for being amongst mankind, but insists that there is a greater world awaiting those who are willing to live properly and in resonance with all creation. It asserts also that, this world and all things in it is are a mere shadow to the existence destined for those who truly believe. It is as an assertion, albeit, that can be proven logically instead of a fanatical stance taken, and is based on facts and not a fabrications by man. Were it not so, the words of true Manifestations and all ideologies They proposed would have perished with Their deaths. As we see, such words are mother to many a civilization and survive time, where other philosophies soon find abandonment with time. This is fact. All known and existent civilizations have a religion as a backbone to the society that worships, as a safeguard to moral and ethical conduct. The human race has survived time because of these principles which have avoided the race of man extinguishing itself entirely...

Our positive lives depend on a life beyond this, and thus we avoid living in an anarchy of no law. All look to rewards for deeds of worth and punishment for deeds of evil. This arrangement is the establishment of a watchdog for all actions of life and has endured time, and is as timeless as our universe seems to be. We hardly can be objective enough for we are caught in subjectivity and know it. None can stand outside the very planet and observe exactly where we are with anything. The best so far we have done universally is to visit our Moon, our satellite, and plant flags, flying there from back to where we are locked in by gravity. Someday we may transcend that but must never forget that the universe is glued together somehow by forces actually unknown to us at this time. With that in mind there lies also the realization that we can only discover the universe if we stay logical. How could it be devoid of a Mind in it? In one way, the universe may not recognize our presence, but it is of the essence that we endeavor to know it more. As the analogy has it, we are as fish who are dependent of the water but know it not. We are dependent on how much we obey His law.

Calling Ourselves to Account

We all know ourselves better than we know anyone else. For this reason, the Holy Books tell us to look to our own actions before concerning ourselves with the actions of others. In due course, the Scriptures tell us, we will be called to account for ourselves. For that reason we should reflect upon our actions and seek always to improve ourselves.

What happens if we do not do so? We end up living thoughtlessly, perhaps not knowing why we are doing anything. We may not even have any real sense of right and wrong, only of what gets us what we want. Thoughtless living is far more likely to lead us away from God than towards Him and from the goal of fulfilling the purpose of our existence because we are to develop to a perfection limited only by our being human in a concrete environment which takes in, not only our physical but also the invisible features of our existence. The description for man once offered is that the human is concrete manifestation in the physical form of an invisible essence. As beings we have to be aware of our deeds because our future progress is to dependent on them. We should be able to look back and says that we did make progress from point one to point two. Humans are not static but dynamic in thinking. If we take in also the existence of a Being that is Perfection itself to a degree we cannot even encompass, and we intend emulate that perfection, then we should be aware that there is a time we have to measure just how far we have come in that effort. Each person is endowed with a capacity to manifest the perfections of God to the extent that being is granted by Him. All things in existence manifest His glory, but upon man has been showered the capacity to manifest that Being to the greatest extent than any other created thing. Much of what we say or know comes from a Representative of that Being, Who can manifest His virtues much more perfectly than any being could. Hence our progress depends on Them and Their Laws. And our nearness to God is measured by our nearness to Them. Such an approach avoids an assertion that we are impotent in achieving that goal. at At the end of the earthly life we are faced with how much we have done to keep within the track of those laws. When we view that in that sense,then we can think of how we can account on how much we have put in this effort of developing our potential. People have called it judgment day, and I call it meeting our destiny ss determined by how much we have striven to achieve that destiny. Failing there, does not reverse life so that we can try again, for we only live in this world once. There seems to be the problem that we cannot go back and correct anything. That then should be hellish in the least! If the Deity decides not to forgive me, for not having tried, how long will it take before I am forgiven and what will it take to gain forgiveness for my failure when I had been grated the opportunity to act? And how will I consciously catch up with myself so that I am at a point of vantage in relationship to my own progress if I am given a chance to progress which I had earlier? Will I ever be able to see as others see, those who have striven and to an extent, won? Will I know the things I am supposed to know or have learned in my life? In that lies a lot of pain. Perhaps that is what the Holy Books call Hell! For there I might pine away waiting not for reward, but mercy, for I had the chance and flitted it away irreversibly! So Bahá'u'lláh says::

43. O SON OF BEING!

**Make mention of Me on My earth,
that in My heaven I may remember thee,
thus shall Mine eyes and thine be solaced.**

(The Arabic Hidden Words)

We are, in the Writings of the Bahá'í Faith, cautioned to look at our faults and not fashion our behavior blindly on that of others with no sense of some knowledge why they do what they do, or the advantage thereof. Bahá'u'lláh insists that we take our lives in hand and be able to account for them. It is in a sense a way of creating responsibility in all our actions. Many times we are also advised to meditate on all words we utter and deeds we perform. This may men meditating on the day's actions each day and seeing how far those might have deviated from the ruling of the Book:

31. O SON OF BEING!

Bring thyself to account each day ere thou art summoned to a reckoning; for death, unheralded, shall come upon thee and thou shalt be called to give account for thy deeds.

(Bahá'u'lláh, The Arabic
Hidden Words)

For the faith of no man can be conditioned by any one except himself.

(Bahá'u'lláh, Gleanings from the
Writings of Bahá'u'lláh, p. 143)

To quote all the things the Blessed Beauty outlines on this theme would fill a book, so I would rather explain from a personal perspective than quote the whole Book.

Each person knows why that particular person chooses a line of action. Such a decision is dependent upon the person, the circumstance and what knows of whatever is said in the Writ about he action. and any other outer influences that person knows. The action has to be based on something. The important thing then is the assurance that the grounding on which the action is based is sure and will not shift after the action is carried out. There, for a believer, even for the Bahá'í who is also a believer, actions must be very close to the Law believed to be sure and correct in foundation. To me this means that when one has options of actions one should choose the action closets to the Law of God. For, with the law is the sure foundation for action. Then it is wise to search for the Law by one's self and believe in that which the mind can account for, and not that which another mind believes or forces on another. That would be then be seen as spiritual responsibility The person has a a frame of reference good enough to handle such decisions. Bahá'ís today depend on Bahá'í Law for it deals with issues of the day. To quote again would be unfair for this is just a person to person advice and not an assertion. One should be able to tabulate why one took an action and not always be unaware why that action was taken, for in the depth of the heart one knows why. This is the reason meditation is so good, because then one can go to depths about all questions and actions executed in a n abstracted way or obstructed way, so that one is not only consciously aware of the why but also acknowledges the how..So, claiming to be 'unconscious ' of taking an action is no safe option! Deep down the heart knows, and this has to be brought to the surface, perhaps though many complexities, but the reality is that one knows.

It is also a good possibility that one can come to a realization of a bad action one has taken. One can always consciously ask for forgiveness. Once that action of prayer is achieved an avowal not to repeat the action taken in the same way, then one becomes a good teacher to those who might chance to come to the same kind of problem without malice or the 'I told you so ' attitude which helps very little in easing pain afterwards. That attitude would be conducive to living in peace with the self,,instead of living the guilt that someone knows the action taken and might hold it against one, subtly or not! Our God is a Living and Forgiving God, only we must own up. One does not forgive one who does not even recognize a wrong committed. We have to be sensitive to ourselves and sensitive to pain in others. In business we utter the words " How can I help you?", very often but fail to execute this in friendly day to day action with friends and neighbors. It seems only a way of saying " I know more about it than you do!". That is no way to look at life, for abrasive it is...

The road to true living is not through preaching distantly about right and wrong, but through a life that is an example to others. First they will observe you act, then they will try to find if your attitude works in real life, and if they do, the battle is half won, because now, if they venture, they may ask how you do that, But that question does not have to be direct in order to give you the conscious idea of being superior, for people do not like to feel inferior to you, not in a society of freedom and free minds! This then is where true symbolic talk comes in. For that way one gives advice, for advice itself and not self aggrandizement. Only God will know what one has done, and He keeps secrets, perhaps "Until you meet!"..

In the days of computers one wonders in what kind

of chip He holds all these memories, but then ask how He made the universe! We simply do not know how, but He does ask to be worshipped with deeds of faith above all else. That would be legitimate. For what a Mind would create the creation but a Mind I have to acclaim as Great and far Superior to any I may know! In any team one likes to know there is a good star, and He is some Star! Always bearing in mind that we speak of the Manifestation and not Him, for He remains Unknowable…

As a boy I read a book which made me laugh very hard. It was called " "God loves Laughter". For the first time in years I could laugh about my own search for truth.

It is funny but serious to know that where I stand generations of men once flourished and I stand on that dust. Is it also in my food? Do I laugh at cannibals and say " I would not do that?" when sheep are made of that same sterner stuff buried in vegetables! Reprocessed bodies! The one thing that is not, is my soul, for it learns different from my parents, for I am a combination of both and not one or the other.; my genes differ, but as a human I am the same as they are, just flesh!

I toy around with the idea of getting to the Next World: Supposing I play all my life, might that not land me in after life of everlastingly playing? That usually wakens me to doing something useful, that He might like, rather than playing all that eighty years. There is accounting to do!

The Bread that is Life

In the Lord's Prayer, Jesus instructed us to pray that God will give us our "daily bread." Outwardly this signifies material sustenance, but I have often wondered if there might be deeper meaning. In studying the *Kitáb-i-Íqán*, I have become convinced that indeed there is.

Bread, the food called "the stuff of life," can be seen as a symbol for spiritual sustenance. In the Old Testament, manna is said to have fallen from Heaven. This can be understood in several ways: God's grace, His teachings and laws, and the Manifestations of God themselves. In sum, religion is that form of bread necessary for man's development through the ages. This "bread" is never withheld from us, and we must always be grateful for it because through it the integrity of the human race is preserved.

The symbolism is perhaps most powerfully expressed in the Last Supper, where Jesus compares His own body and blood, which were about to be sacrificed for us—to bread and wine. The spiritual sustenance we obtain from the Manifestation of God comes at the cost of His suffering and often His physical death—suffering and death ironically meted out by our own hands. At first we refuse the spiritual food that God has sent us, but in the end it is the cause of our salvation and progress through all the worlds of God.

We offer many excuses for this rejection, but ultimately it may boil down to our inability to see our own needs and our own best advantage. We cling to old ways and to whatever gratifies our physical needs, oblivious to our spiritual needs and the needs of the age in which we live. Yet the heavenly bread, our sustenance over the centuries, is never denied us, and in time we learn to appreciate it. Without this guidance, we would live in anarchy. All our norms and customs are derived from it. We live and depend upon its revelation throughout history. Although it may not be obvious because the fact is obscured by the passage of centuries, without the bread that is religion the very cohesiveness of our societies would fail. In this regard, the laws of God are also like the ocean, as the passage below suggests and we as the fish. We may find an excuse to disregard the ocean, but as fish, our lives depend entirely on its existence and sustenance.

> **Indeed, the laws of God are like unto the ocean and the children of men as fish, did they but know it.**

> (The Kitab-i-Aqdas, p. 5)

The bread from God comes at all seasons for the upkeep of the development of humankind and to ascertain that correct attitudes and understandings are maintained as we head for further life in all His worlds, which are numberless.,.. the very reason Jesus speaks of the many mansions of the Father. It is however, up to each soul to reach and consume this bread, and none is forced, for the existence of God is not dependent upon our acceptance of Him or the bread. But He loves us and wishes us to progress according to His intention for His creation in which man is he representative of Himself as the image, and of His qualities when he obeys and consumes the bread, the religion itself as manifested its laws. Refusal is not proof of the failure of its efficacy and can be to our detriment as we progress through the years, if we progress at all. As Lord of Existence, His Kingdom is not limited to us, and He can well dispense with all things, but He has reasons why He created His creation and made man, as Bahá'ís say, " to know Him and to worship Him" (Noon Day Prayer of Bahá'ís in " Bahá'í Prayers") This bread is no less than the religion of God by which God feeds us and directs us as we live in this earthly life. It descends upon us at all seasons, much as the manna among the Israelis as they left Egypt for the Land of the Promise. This is the 'bread f lie' spoken of in the Writings that is so necessary for us to achieve developing towards being His Image.

Music

When I read in the *Kitáb-i-Íqán* of the "melodies of Jesus, Son of Mary, sung in the Ridvan (Paradise) of the Gospels," for the first time I connected divine Revelation with song. There are more examples of this in the Bahá'í Writings and other Scriptures. For example, Bah'áu'lláh used birdsong, particularly of the nightingale and the dove, as metaphors for revelation. So it is worth considering song for a moment as a manifestation of revelation. In scriptural writings of Christianity one can often think of the "Songs of David" which are a major part of the praise of God in the Bible..In the Arabic and Persian texts of Bahá'í Writings one often sees the terms " Bolboleh" (nightingale)"or "Vargat'ul Firdaus " (Nightingale of Paradise) quite often. We can also consider that the Book of Hindus called the *Baghavad Gita* means " The Celestial Song", etc. Even a normal musical song can be used to deliver messages. Imagine where we would be without the songs of Homer in history!

Songs can be written praising God or glorifying immoral behavior. Musicians can live moral or immoral lives, for a song sung by anyone is itself no proof of purity of motive in that person. Even the beauty of the notes does not even indicate the pure meaning of the words of a song. Many times songs are sung deliberately to cause indignity or degradation on one person or another. In this vein a person can listen to a divine tune and plan evil at that same time. So the sound of the music is no criteria for purity of motive. In order have a love song, therefore it has to be sung to the beloved in praise or appreciation, rather than the appreciation of the notes. Songs of evil have been known to have beautiful notes. The music itself is not the song, but how the words thrill the heart is the song. For, as religion is a song, it is the effect of its words on the heart and soul of man that produce ecstasy of heart, and not the notes or what it sounds like when chanted or sung. In order to listen with the heart, the mind has to have an understanding,otherwise such music is meaningless. That is why some musicians choose not to sing " I love you" all the time, but to put in some other useful message into the song. The attraction of the notes should cause one to know what the song is all about and why it is sung. Without this angle, anything goes! If one uses the French phrase: " Chantez mois une chanson" then one has to know that the song has to be pleasing to the hearer, so when David sings songs about the Lord, they enchant those who love the Lord, and nonbelievers themselves remain unimpressed. If then the Manifestations want to sing songs of the Lord, the Lord is the Celestial and not earthly,not because of the sound of he notes, but really the mystery of the words and the sound thereof. That is music for the heart and the soul. For the soul is the mystery of God in creation. Hence Bahá'u'lláh mentions that " Man is my mystery and I am His mystery" in the Writings of the Bahá'ís:

All these names and attributes are applicable to him. Even as He hath said: "Man is My mystery, and I am his mystery.

(The Kitab-i-Iqan, p. 101)

We put the songs of David in notes, and not that they already are in notes. So, the song is the One sung About! We deliver it in notes. This is because those songs are a praise of our Creator and through them we learn of Him Who is the Eternal Song, the Celestial Song sung in all the Scriptures....

Religion or the declaration thereof has to be listened to with both heart and mind, so that it makes sense to both. The heart without the mind is no proof, but when combined the two do make sense. The mind without the heart is also no proof of a religion for religion is best manifested with both mind and heart. To say "I believe" is a good song, but to perform belief is a reality of the belief, otherwise it remains a thought unexpressed,... a deed never done. To have a book on shelf does not prove that one has read it.

To sing to the beloved is to extol the virtues of the beloved, but the actual deed that manifests undying love is necessary. My mind always devolves on a thought on Carton in the "Tale of Two Cities" (Outlet Book Company p. 848) who dies at the guillotine for the sake of a love. The greatest being is that of one offering a life for an intended good that lasts ages when achieved. Without this life is meaningless and lacks lustre. Many of those who died in Persia during the Bahá'í persecutions died with a song in their hearts, for they knew that, by that sacrifice, they had not just achieved the highest good but had served generations of humankind. Recognition of this is not dependent on recognition by man, but by the intent in the soul is recorded in the Eternal, expressed to the public or not. That is song! As my friend once said that the life of a man is like a song and once the song is broken it has to be continued exactly where it left off. This theme has been repeated many times in sundry lives.

Religion is a song ideally sung to please humankind that He has remembered His love for man. He has enormous love which he can only express to a very limited extent due to the regular failure of man to understand, and the measure of his growth in each era. Thus Bahá'u'lláh speaks of the many songs the nightingale cannot and does not sing until an appointed time, and Jesus speaks of the many things He could have said were man prepared to listen. This is the essence of the promise and to which when not understood becomes as a kind of personal damnation or condemnation by the self. It is a hellish thing to be promised good and fail to rise up to the promise later! It should be like: " Hark! I hear the sound of many waters again!"

It has been mentioned in themes on the universe, that the planets as they rotate must emit a sound, and this has been likened to the song of the universe. As always, none hear the song for there is much interruption around us, and the almost deafening sound of the songs emitted by that universe is lost to the ear. There is a book I once chanced to read called " The Song of the Spheres' whose title I loved but which I never delved deeply into, however my understanding was that planets sing as they turn, but who hears this sound? It has also been conjectured as a popular thought that music comes from the celestial spheres, but proof of this lacks. But we do know the song of Holiness in our lives emanating from the sayings of purity from Holy Words which cause ecstasy of heart and soul, and fire us to deeds of spiritual and physical valor for the Cause of God,, and we sing those with our lives in life spans of sacrifice, measured in time, but lasting many years as examples of purity. There are men and women who have expressed this theme of sacrifice even in normal history, with their lives and asked for no reward. One example I have of such is that of Jean d'Arc or the so called Joan of Arc.

Having come to this realization then it is the heart expressing itself that matters rather than the notes of a song. It is also obvious that music does not have to be comprised of many complex notes, but can in essence be in fewer notes where the heart is still active in the expression. It is worthy to consider that,music being a thing of the heart, can be expressed anywhere, from complex cities to middles of jungles and still be music. That is not logic but a reality. For we have such music from many parts in the world which we have incorporated in different notes into what we now call " our music". and which was no more than a few notes at its inception. To deny this would be to deny our own history that we never ever lived in jungles and produced, still music at its best expression of attracting the heart. If we produce such songs of love, how much more can we express love and music by our lives? Lives of purity must be adored by the words, in whatever notes we place them. That is song!

Coming to this pinnacle of understanding, it does not really matter what heart "lives" the song.. ;if it is a song of love it is acceptable to any heart, especially if that song is expressed as an act of love. It does not matter then, in the myriads of languages the earth has, what language the song is sung in, if it is an expression of,love. In my music collection I have songs ranging from Africa to Russia with all nations in between and I love them all, especially when I learn that they are songs of love. That being the case, what does it matter then what language produces a song of truth? Can I disdain the song that thrills my heart with its words, if the words are life giving? Can we disdain a song because of it's singer, and not the words!

So, Thomas Gray says:" Full many a flower is born to blush unseen

And waste its sweetness upon the desert air"(Tyfeld,, Thomas Grey,Elegy, p.60) For many a song sung is never to be heard. Many of us acknowledge God but rejected those songs sung by Jesus and yet Bahá'u'lláh mentions in His Day the songs sung by Jesus in His time. Jesus Himself invited all to partake of His Word, in a parable of the Party arranged for the rich which they failed to attend:

> **These are the melodies, sung by Jesus, Son of Mary, in accents of majestic power in the Ridvan of the Gospel, revealing those signs that must needs herald the advent of the Manifestation after Him**

> (Bahá'u'lláh, The Kitab-i-Iqan, p. 24)

> **But the falcon of the mystic heaven hath many a wondrous carol of the spirit in His breast, and the Persian bird keepeth in His soul many a sweet Arab**

melody; yet these are hidden, and hidden shall remain.

(The Seven Valleys, p. 28)

The Fulfillment of Prophecy

According to the Blessed Beauty, there is a difference between Prophets who are "endowed with constancy" and Prophets who are not. Prophets who are endowed with constancy are referred to in the Kitáb-i-Iqán- as those named as Manifestations and They start or begin a new religion and a civilizations which lasts years. They foretell future events with exactness, bring a new book, and name those events, promises., in a definite way. Prophets who are not endowed with constancy are themselves followers of The Major Prophets referred to above as Those Endowed with Constancy. Thus Moses, Jesus, Krishna, Muhammad, Buddha, Zoroaster and many others, not mentioned here and Those of whom we have lost names are part of those Prophets, for according to Bahá'u'lláh religion was with man for longer than is recorded in the Books that we as a generation have.. There are even quotes in the Writings of Bán-u'llálh from poetry. This in turn, means that a poet may write a religious truth without knowing its true meaning but it comes to him or her as inspiration. Whereas a prophet usually knows what they speak of especially the Ones Endowed with Constancy that Bahá'u'lláh mentions in the Writings. Viewed in that sense, it is then possible to have a prophet today if the person is pure enough, and it is possible today for a poet to reveal a spiritual truth even if the poet himself does not view it as such.

> **This, notwithstanding the fact that no eye hath beheld so great an outpouring of bounty, nor hath any ear heard of such a revelation of loving kindness. Such bounty and revelation have been made manifest, that the revealed verses seemed as vernal showers raining from the clouds of the mercy of the All-Bountiful. The Prophets "endowed with constancy," whose loftiness and glory shine as the sun, were each honoured with a Book which all have seen, and the verses of which have been duly ascertained. Whereas the verses which have rained from this Cloud of divine mercy have been so abundant that none hath yet been able to estimate their number. A score of volumes are now available. How many still remain beyond our reach! How many have been plundered and have fallen into the 217 hands of the enemy, the fate of which none knoweth.**

> (Bahá'u'lláh, The Kitab-i-Iqan, p. 216)

> **The mystery enshrined within this verse is now concealed; it will be revealed**

in the year after Hín."[2] The Báb subsequently quoted this well-known tradition: "Treasures lie hidden beneath the throne of God; the key to those treasures is the tongue of poets.

(The Dawn-Breakers, p. 258)

This theme is demonstrated by Bahá'u'lláh as He has quoted both Háfiz and Sa'd, who were Persian poets, in the Writings. It would take many pages to dwell on this as there are several parts both from traditions among men that have poetry quoted in the Writings, but each time Bahá'u'lláh would precede the quote with a statement that it was a from a poet. In this we have to imagine that if we are pure enough we could predict the future in poetry. Otherwise why would this quality be limited to an age among humankind? The mercies of God surround us at all times, it is up to us to use them or be conscious of them, even as prayer is to ask for strength to perform a deed of some good, and not so that one is static,unless being so is a requirement of the problem at hand.

Ordinary persons do not make prophecies, but prophecies are usually made, by trustworthy persons we respect for spiritual insight. After that, we as ordinary people do not consciously fulfill prophecies, but prophecies are fulfilled, always when God is ready that they be fulfilled for the comings and goings of all Manifestations, His Representatives on earth, are all in His Hand and none other's.

The belief of Bahá'ís is that God is One and is no competition against Himself. So, what He tells us to look for is universal in that it has a meaning even if at first we do not see it. It is far better to use the mind and be careful about disputing until we are certain of facts.

There is predetermined time for revelation and none of us know the time or hour of each revelation and it is God's Will that at the time of the revelation we are able to recognize it and believe. The signs mentioned usually are there to be seen. It is we who sometimes refuse to acknowledge them based on what we feel we currently know about a religion.

Baha'ullah in the Kitab-i-Iqan does describe the time of coming and setting of a revelation and makes a number of examples, some of which are: the seasons of the year, the risings and settings of the sun, …. the setting of the sun of a religion and the rising of another. He even describes the time of the night when we are between religions; Kindly, He cautions us and explains prophecies and tells us that He does not wish these things to "agitate the soul and perplex" the mind.

> **Therefore, these sayings which We have quoted in support of Our argument must be attentively considered, that the divergent utterances of the Manifestations of the Unseen and Daysprings of Holiness may cease to agitate the soul and perplex the mind.**
>
> (Bahá'u'lláh, The Kitab-i-Iqan, p. 181)

To a greater or lesser degree, prophecy is part of every religion. Prophecy basically looks forward to future events, frequently portraying them in symbolic language. In some instances, it may be that the author of a prophecy did not himself recognize it as such. King David, for instance, was inspired to write his profound psalms, some of which do indeed look forward to future events. The Manifestations of God have knowledge of all things, and can reveal prophecies in either plain or symbolic language, depending on our level of understanding.

But acknowledging the existence of prophecy is very different from recognizing its fulfillment. Indeed, in some cases it may only be the Manifestations of God who know the correct interpretation of a prophecy. This may be why Bahá'u'lláh spent considerable time on prophetic interpretation in the *Kitáb-i-Íqán*. Nevertheless we can apply our rational powers to examine any interpretations that are offered, and come to some reasonable conclusions about them. Even though religion is fundamentally supernatural in character, it nevertheless has a logic and does not completely overturn the workings of the natural world and works with what we already can comprehend in thought and fair examination.

Adam and Eve

Over the centuries people have read many things into the story of Adam and Eve. Today it is no longer rational to view it as an historical account. It doesn't fit into current anthropological understanding of human prehistory. Clearly, then, it must be taken allegorically rather than literally.

Socially, the story of Adam and Eve has sometimes been used as an excuse for the subjugation of women. Eve, after all, allowed herself to be deluded by the serpent and in turn enticed Adam into sin. Nothing in the Bible lays the blame for humanity's "fall" at the feet of Eve—indeed what references there are speak of Adam's sin, not hers—but this has not prevented such abuses of the story.

'Abdu'l-Bahá gave one interpretation of the Garden of Eden tale and encouraged us to reflect upon it to discover other meanings. I would therefore like to offer a few of my own thoughts on the matter. To begin with, Adam and Eve were given everything on Earth except for one thing, the fruit of the tree of knowledge. They had only to obey this one injunction to remain in paradise, but their nature was to question and test. Why should they be forbidden this one thing? It seemed contrary to reason. And so they disobeyed and through disobedience came to know the difference between good and evil. This knowledge had far-reaching repercussions. No longer virtuous by default, they had to strive for virtue while combating the promptings of a "lower nature" that often directed them away from virtue. Rather than being literally a man and a woman, Adam and Eve represent two aspects of the human reality: mind and heart, spirit and soul. The lower nature is not symbolized by either of them; rather, that is symbolized by the serpent, which prompted them to turn away from God. In listening to our lower nature, we shut ourselves out from God and must engage in search and struggle to attain His presence again.

Again there is nothing in this to suggest that women bear greater culpability than men in our separation from God. Rather it is a story of the human condition, the result of having a moral sense, and the consequences of being ruled by our lower nature. Men and women are spiritual equals, sharing alike in the glories and troubles of human nature. God stands ready to forgive and assist men and women alike, as amply illustrated by a well-known story from the Gospel of St. John:

> **And the scribes and Pharisees brought unto him a woman taken in adultery; and when they had set her in the midst, They say unto him, Master, this woman was taken in adultery, in the very act.**
>
> **Now Moses in the law commanded us, that such should be stoned: but what sayest thou? This they said, tempting him, that they might have to accuse him. But Jesus stooped down, and with his finger wrote on the ground, as though he heard them not.**
>
> **So when they continued asking him, he lifted up himself, and said unto them, He that is without sin among you, let him first cast a stone at her.**
>
> **And again he stooped down, and wrote on the ground.**
>
> **And they which heard it, being convicted by their own conscience, went out one by one, beginning at the eldest, even unto the last: and Jesus was left alone, and the woman standing in the midst.**

**When Jesus had lifted up himself,
and saw none but the woman, he said
unto her, Woman, where are those thine
accusers? hath no man condemned thee?
She said, No man, Lord. And Jesus said
unto her, Neither do I condemn thee: go,
and sin no more.**

(John 8:3-11, KJV)

Today, Bahá'ulláh has explicitly stated that men and women are equal in the sight of God and should be so regarded on Earth, leaving us no excuse to twist the Scriptures of the past into forms that suggest otherwise. This equality is indisputable even though men and women may sometimes play different roles in life. Biology dictates that men are fathers and women are mothers, for example. In the Bahá'í Faith, men have been given the task of serving in the Universal House of Justice, but not owing to any superiority of men over women. Women can and do serve in every other capacity.

As Bahá'ís we know that 'Abdu'l-Baha, the Center of the Covenant appointed Lua Getsinger as Herald to the Covenant of the Faith, a command which applied to Bahá'ís, the world over. Lua was one of the believers in the early days in the United States.

After the Master had left this world, Shoghi Effendi His eldest grandson was made, according to His Covenant the Guardian of the Faith of Bahá'u'lláh. However, before taking up office as the Guardian, Shoghi Effendi, in order to recuperate from the shock of the loss of a Grandfather, and that of being appointed Guardian,left his grandaunt to be the head the Bahá'í' Faith for the period of his absence from Haifa, Israel.

We can also reflect on why one of the first eighteen believers in the Bábi, Faith which preceded the Bahá'í Revelation, was a woman and a poetess.

The statement from the Center of the Covenant stands without doubt clear that " Men and women are equal".

It seems one of the jokes on us is that both men and women are born of woman. It sounds very unreasonable to imagine that the Deity at each birth is going to assign a destiny. None is ever sure what sex the baby will be. It would even find an illogical incomprehensible explanation to find out how we are to determine sins of those who,later in life change their sexual orientation.

Biologists insist that the parts in the woman are manifest in the man, though appearing as if atrophied but they are there as evidence that the case and sex could have been otherwise.

To my mother it was very simple: "You do any work I give you and never tell me it is a woman's job!"

We are made with expertise on both sides, and have to recognize that. Each in the final analysis serves a vital purpose in life. This age of Bahá'u'lláh has to examine this keenly to see how adaptation to the environment has given us tools in both sexes to achieve this purpose.

When boys are circumcised in order to become recognized as men in societies in Africa, they have to recognize that the stricture of having to bleed is to, once in life, to emulate their mothers and their sisters, so that they never get to trivialize birth and what goes with it. They are reminded that when you go to the toilet, you have to squat as your sister does, so that you experience what she has to go through in her situation and never find it to be any less than a man's, Hence today, the major part in improving this custom has been championed by doctors who are of the female sex in the Cape Province of South Africa. These are mere facts but the injunction from the Cause of Bahá'u'lláh was issued long ago the 1800s as a declaration. I do not see my genes separating into those of a woman and those of men. Surely they truly equally contribute to what I have become.

Shakespeare has said that: No one can comprehend the configuration of the mind from the face

> **There is no art**
> **To find the mind's construction in**
> **he face**.

(Van Doren Stern, 140)

How do I see the smallness or greatness in sins in men and women then just because the outward shape is different?. Do I know any inward strengths at all? Thus, Jean d'Arc died!.. after fighting a bitter battle with men was declared one possessed with sorcery and her strengths to be no more than magic, when magic is no more than the sleight of the hand and not reality! Her transformation into a fighting force was trivialized after she had won the bitter battle for her country to be nothing but sorcery and her body consigned to flames!

Creation

Creation has often been imagined as a one-time event, occurring at "the beginning of time," but God cannot be so limited. As a Creator, He must always be creating and must always have a creation. Likewise if God is the Sovereign of Eternity, He must eternally have had subjects and will continue to have subjects.

In a very real sense, the coming of a Manifestation of God is a divine act of creation. Through the influence of the Word, all things are made new: a new race of men arises, a new civilization is created, new "stars" are lit in the "heavens." For humanity, each Manifestation of God is a new end and a new beginning, yet in a larger sense we stand neither at the beginning nor at the end. We have inhabited this Earth for tens of thousands of years, and 'Abdu'l-Baha indicated that the religious cycle inaugurated by the Báb would last for 500,000 years to come. During this time other Manifestations of God will appear, but only at its end will we come to a full circle and a new cycle begin. Thus, humanity has a long future stretching ahead of it.

In a physical sense none know the top or bottom of the universe, or if what we think is the top is actually the bottom. The universe itself is enveloped in a thick darkness all alleviated only by its suns. Thus this becomes a manifestation of our spiritual world which is very dark unless illuminated by the Holy Ones, the Manifestations of the virtues of God.

In view of God being Creator and in view of the fact that we do not know the foundations of creation or even the universe, we have to admit that it can have no end, but has the end that it is not the world we go to when we transcend death, into another world of being. This view highlights the necessity to develop in this world and thus be able to survive with whatever we might have at death in the next.

Yes, we can be, as religionists assert, in a disputed ideology, that there is life after death, but who is certain of this when none of us have died and come back?

It may be impossible, for anyone to travel the whole universe and come back, but we learn from observation that there are things we have to know exist without a physical and direct experience thereof. An example of that, is knowing that the sun is hot from a distance without nearing it and having to burn in its light, for then I could never come back to prove that. The dreams I have which come true to a detail tell me there is some way I travel the future while I am in the present. My question is how does the future come to the present in my dreams if the mystery of life is as simple as some people claim?

Through the years there have been prophecies that I have read about in the Holy Books, of events that do take place in time. Can I go ahead and disbelieve this with that evidence and still hold that my own history books are true? What would be my supportive reasoning?

The saying goes:

I was a hidden mystery and desired to be known, therefore I created the creation in order to be known.

I have found such short statements useful in trying to determine the truth about existence.:

I was a Hidden Treasure. I wished to be made known, and thus I called creation into being in order that I might be known.

(The Kitab-i-Aqdas, p. 174)

15. O SON OF UTTERANCE!

Turn thy face unto Mine and renounce all save Me; for My sovereignty endureth and My dominion perisheth not. If thou seekest another than Me, yea, if thou searchest the universe for evermore, thy quest will be in vain.

(The Arabic Hidden Words)

The believer would do well to combine faith with reason in this issue. The self will in time when it raises the question of: Why am I here? Even though the hustle and bustle of the day may cause it to recede into the unconscious. The sober moments of the day will sometime or other raise it. To quote all Writings in the issue would not be the intention of the author, for he would rather write from the perspective of what and all this has caused him to have understanding of the question involved without having to complicate it. It is fact that we live in darkness, both physically and otherwise, and are in need of guidance, but guidance has to be trusted in order to be observed as true. Science has that all is teleological, where religion says that we shall subsist. One comes from our deductive ability, and the other from a source we know not but have learned to trust through worship in all the years. Which then shall it be?

There have been many a theory about existence but all the men and women who propounded these have passed on.

A man of science learns from experiments performed for years and cannot foresee the future, and a man of religion, devoid of all learning, through prayer finds the future and writes it down. Somehow the two must "pull the wagon together", otherwise pandemonium waits and lurks in all corners of existence. We keep asking: Who were these people who are in all civilizations and always speak of future events that come true? And again we ask: why did we not believe the people who proposed that the sun and earth were round?

It is also wise to watch for the bats of night, for when night descends they become active. When guidance is ignored they find answers and all those answers are wrong, for their love is of darkness, and not light which is true guidance. We have had many a proponent who has come feigning to give light when self interest was the main theme.

However, if then a person, be they a man or a woman, gives himself up in a quest for answers, and never aspire to all the things we desire for ourselves in our earthly life,, and claims that he does this for love of God and humankind, surely we have to take some pain in asking the origins of his or her thinking. Guidance will not always come from one sex or from one of a certain age or station in life! The nobility of spirit has no sex.

13. O SON OF SPIRIT!

I created thee rich, why dost thou bring thyself down to poverty? Noble I made thee, wherewith dost thou abase thyself? Out of the essence of knowledge I gave thee being, why seekest thou enlightenment from anyone beside Me? Out of the clay of love I molded thee, how dost thou busy thyself with another?

Turn thy sight unto thyself, that thou mayest find Me standing within thee, mighty, powerful and self-subsisting.

(The Arabic Hidden Words)

**Split the atom's heart, and lo!
Within it thou wilt find a sun. [1]
[1 Persian mystic poem.]**

(Bahá'u'lláh, The Seven Valleys, p. 12)

The first is His statement: "O My Servant! Obey Me and I shall make thee like unto Myself. I say 'Be,' and it is, and thou shalt say 'Be,' and it shall be."

And the second: "O Son of Adam! Seek fellowship with none until thou hast found Me, and whenever thou shalt long for Me, thou shalt find Me close to thee."

(Bahá'u'lláh, The Four Valleys, p. 63)

Somehow the human must find the underlying power within himself to solve the mystery, for He has not said the universe is My image but does say: Thou art My image!

First of all, he is made in the image of God, in the likeness of the Supernal Light, even as the Torah saith, 'Let

us make man in our image, after our likeness.'[1] This divine image betokeneth all the qualities of perfection whose lights, emanating from the Sun of Truth, illumine the realities of men. And among the greatest of these attributes of perfection are wisdom and knowledge. Ye must therefore put forth a mighty effort, striving by night and day and resting not for a moment, to acquire an abundant share of all the sciences and arts, that the Divine Image, which shineth out from the Sun of Truth, may illumine the mirror of the hearts of men.

[1 Genesis 1:26]. 141

(Selections from the Writings of Abdu'l-Baha, p. 140)

The first is His statement: "O My Servant! Obey Me and I shall make thee like unto Myself. I say 'Be,' and it is, and thou shalt say 'Be,' and it shall be."

And the second: "O Son of Adam! Seek fellowship with none until thou hast found Me, and whenever thou shalt long for Me, thou shalt find Me close to thee."

(The Seven Valleys and the Four Valleys, p. 63)

Witness the wondrous evidences of God's handiwork, and reflect upon its range and character. He Who is the Seal of the Prophets hath said: "Increase my wonder and amazement at Thee, O God!"

(Gleanings from the Writings of Bahá'u'lláh, p. 162)

Our strange surroundings

Dark and cold are intrinsic properties of our universe. Gazing into space, we find a vast wasteland of nothingness, punctuated here and there by blazes of heat and light. But the stars, though numerous, are on the whole very far apart, and between the filament-like collections of galaxies we find enormous voids. Our own world, rotating once every twenty four hours, passes through alternating cycles of light and dark. The polar opposites of light and dark, and related to them, of heat and cold, are so familiar to us that most of us scarcely think about them except to the degree to which they affect our immediate comfort and security.

But this very familiarity makes these aspects of our existence perfect symbols for the opposites in our emotional, intellectual, and moral lives. We speak of goodness, knowledge, happiness, and peace as light, while evil, ignorance, sorrow and war are darkness. We display our goodness in the "full light of day," but hide our misdeeds in the darkness of the "closet." Not surprisingly, we find this symbolism in the Holy Writings of all religions. For example in the *Fire Tablet*, Bahá'u'lláh says, **"The universe is darkened with the dust of sin"**

(*Bahá'í Prayers*, p. 218).

No wonder then, that the Bahá'í Writings speak of those times when religion erodes and the guidance of most of its leaders falters as a spiritual nighttime. No wonder that they speak of the Manifestation of God as "the Sun of Reality" whose coming is the "dawn" of a new age.

Departure from the divine Law brings with it true darkness. It affects how we live in deed and in word. Moreover, when the guardians of the light—religious and spiritual leaders—fall into darkness, souls seeking the eternal light no longer know where to turn to find it. But God does not leave us long in this condition for at such a time when religion is eclipsed, He sends His Manifestation to bring us back into the brilliant light of a new Day.

There are quotes of this issue in many Holy Writings, and it is not fair to test and tire minds by making all quotes available without one necessarily explaining one's stand on the issue. One expects that after reading others will find cause to seek more answers for themselves in each case and be able to determine that darkness of the soul mentioned, through the performance of unholy works, is worse than the darkness of the universe. Yet, we might know that without the "Suns of Divine Truth" we would not know where we stand with our Creator and be stunted in spiritual growth.

It is wise then to look for the light of His word in all things once darkness descends on us, with the falling of all stars and moons of guidance into the mire of sinfulness and loss of divine light.

The Great and the Small

We find many other symbols for spiritual reality in the physical universe. Consider the size of the universe and those things that inhabit it. Human beings are often regarded as puny, insignificant, little more than a fortuitous little accident in the immensity of an uncaring cosmos. Yet surely our physical size is not our measure. We are spiritual and intellectual creatures unlike any others we have yet found. Some believe that we may never find life anywhere but on Earth, much less advanced intelligence such as we possess. The entire universe is folded up within us, encompassed by both our physical makeup and our intellectual capacity. There are methods advanced to tap into that source that is in humans. The most important aim for the whole of creation is in man and true religion.

> **WORSHIP thou God in such wise that if thy worship lead thee to the fire, no alteration in thine adoration would be produced, and so likewise if thy recompense should be paradise. Thus and thus alone should be the worship which befitteth the one True God. Shouldst thou worship Him because of fear, this would be unseemly in the sanctified**

Court of His presence, and could not be regarded as an act by thee dedicated to the Oneness of His Being. Or if thy gaze should be on paradise, and thou shouldst worship Him while cherishing such a hope, thou wouldst make God›s creation a partner with Him, notwithstanding the fact that paradise is desired by men.

(Selections from the Writings of the Báb, p. 77)

Consider these passages from Bahá'u'lláh's Writings, which speak of humanity generally and the exalted station of the Manifestations of God, the "Perfect Man":

"Lauded be Thy name, O Lord my God! I testify that Thou wast a hidden Treasure wrapped within Thine immemorial Being and an impenetrable Mystery enshrined in Thine own Essence. Wishing to reveal Thyself, Thou didst call into being the Greater and the Lesser Worlds, and didst choose Man above all Thy creatures, and didst make Him a sign of both of these worlds, O Thou Who art our Lord, the Most Compassionate!"

(Prayers and Meditations of Bahá'u'lláh, p. 48)

"But for Thee, I would not have created the spheres."

(Kitáb-i-Iqán, p.171)

"Through His potency the Trees of Divine Revelation have yielded their fruits, every one of which hath been sent down in the form of a Prophet, bearing a Message to God's creatures in each of the worlds whose number God, alone, in His all-encompassing Knowledge, can reckon. This He hath accomplished through the agency of but one Letter of His Word, revealed by His Pen -- a Pen moved by His directing Finger -- His Finger itself sustained by the power of God's Truth."

(Gleanings from the Writings of Bahá'u'lláh, p. 104)

Hell

When I was a child, my parents taught me of a good angel and a bad angel in constant conflict, whispering to me on matters of right and wrong. Like all the kids in my neighborhood, I was taught to fear the punishment of hell in the afterlife.

Before I turned twelve and was confirmed in the

Anglican Church, I attended church each morning between 6:00 a.m. and 7:00 a.m., Monday through Thursday. (Friday was reserved for the English Service and Saturday for preparation for communion.) As an altar server, I would help the priest prepare for communion. One of the psalms we prayed together was:

> **Judge me, O God, and plead my cause against an ungodly nation: O deliver me from the deceitful and unjust man.**
>
> **For thou art the God of my strength: why dost thou cast me off? Why go I mourning because of the oppression of the enemy?**
>
> **O send out thy light and thy truth: let them lead me; let them bring me unto thy holy hill, and to thy tabernacles.**
>
> **Then will I go unto the altar of God, unto God my exceeding joy: yea, upon the harp will I praise thee, O God my God.**

(Holy Bible, Psalms 43:1-4, KJV)

At that same time, in school we were assigned some poems to memorize. I remember them to this day and quote them here because they reflect my own thinking:

We are but Minutes

We are but minutes—little things
Each one furnished with sixty wings,

With which we fly on our unseen track,
And not a minute ever comes back.

We are but minutes—yet each one bears
A little burden of joys and cares,
Patiently take the minutes of pain,
The worst of minutes cannot remain.

We are but minutes—when we bring
A few of the drops from pleasure's spring,
Taste their sweetness while we stay,
It takes but a minute to fly away.

We are but minutes—use us well,
For how we are used we must one day tell,
Who uses us has hours to use,
Who loses minutes whole years must lose.

(Author anonymous. The poem dates
to c. 1880. Set to music, it was published
in several editions by D. Appleton-Century
Co. in *The Hymnal for Boys and Girls*, edited
by Caroline Bird Parker & G. Darlington
Richards, where it appears as #112.)

The Beggar Maid

Her arms across her breast she laid;
She was more fair than words can say;
Barefooted came the beggar maid;
Before the king Cophetua
In robe and crown the king stept down,

To meet and greet her on her way;
'It is no wonder' said the lords,
'She is more beautiful than day.'

As shines the moon in clouded skies,
She in her poor attire was seen;
One praised her ankles and her eyes,
One her dark hair and lovesome mien.
So sweet a face, and angel grace,
In all that land had ever been.
Cophetua swore a royal oath:
'This beggar maid shall be my queen!'
(Alfred, Lord Tennyson. "The Beggar Maid",
1842.)

The first poem speaks of us as moments in time, passing by yet linked together and never forgotten. Tennyson's seems to see us as the essence of poverty yet enriched by a beauty that raises us to royalty. The Psalm and the poems all speak of us as both small and great, both nothing and everything. This, I have come to see, is bound up with the content of our lives and our ultimate fate.

Heaven, you see, is reward. Hell is punishment. Both are promised in the Holy Books, but there is a difference. Heaven can be obtained either through God's justice (as a reward for a good life) or His mercy (what He gives us out of love, even though we don't deserve it). Hell can only be our fate through His justice. In this tension between justice and mercy lies the source of much theology.

The question of punishment once occupied me more than reward or mercy. After all, hell is often envisioned as a place of fire and torment. It's not a pleasant thought, especially if one thinks of it as an eternal condition from which there is no escape! It may not be surprising that so much attention seems to be given to hellfire and damnation. But is that kind of punishment—eternal agony—really just?

Bahá'u'lláh answered the question in a different manner. While upholding what the Holy Books of the past said, He cast them in a new light: heaven is reunion with God, while hell is separation from Him. Further, the "fire" of hell arises not from any torment imposed upon the sinner, but because the sinner, at the moment of death, becomes aware of his spiritual state and of all the things that have escaped him as a result of his own choices and actions. One should not think of this as some watered-down version of hell: it is indeed a "fire" and a "torment." But it is a natural consequence of a person's failure to live as God intended us to live, just as skinned knees are a natural consequence of carelessness on a concrete surface.

It is much like the final scene of *Doctor Faustus*, in which the great Elizabethan dramatist Christopher Marlowe gives Faustus these lines: This partly is also manifest in Goethe's " Faust". Goethe was a philosopher at the time of the evolution of the liberal and national revolts in Europe,and being in a higher class than his contemporary, Schiller, he concentrated in theme of hell and heaven while Schiller dealt more with 'workers' and such concerns. Hence the reference to heaven and hell in the story, and differences of commitment in that issue:

FAUSTUS: God forbade it, indeed; but
Faustus hath done it: for vain pleasure of

> twenty-four years hath Faustus lost eternal
> joy and felicity. I writ them a bill with mine
> own blood: the date is expired: the time will
> come, and he will fetch me.
>
> (Marlowe, p.135)

This is perhaps why Bahá'u'lláh tells us to call ourselves to account each day, before we are summoned to a reckoning. But God is also merciful. He knows we are not perfect. He knows that we will stumble and fall from time to time. I think that if, when summoned to our reckoning, we can admit our weaknesses but also honestly say that we tried, God will likely forgive us. Those who have passed into the next life may also be assisted through the prayers of others who have not, and through good works performed in their names, to find such forgiveness. Even those who face His justice may hope for His mercy. Even hell does not have to be a permanent sentence. Since none of us has stood before His judgment, I can only quote the following for others to see and make their own decisions:

> **If, in the Day when all the peoples
> of the earth will be gathered together,
> any man should, whilst standing in the
> presence of God, be asked: "Wherefore
> hast thou disbelieved in My Beauty and
> turned away from My Self," and if such a
> man should reply and say: "Inasmuch as
> all men have erred, and none hath been
> found willing to turn his face to the
> Truth, I, too, following their example,**

have grievously failed to recognize the Beauty of the Eternal," such a plea will, assuredly, be rejected. For the faith of no man can be conditioned by any one except himself.

(Baha'u'llah, Gleanings from the
Writings of Baha'u'llah, p. 143)

31. O SON OF BEING!

Bring thyself to account each day ere thou art summoned to a reckoning; for death, unheralded, shall come upon thee and thou shalt be called to give account for thy deeds.

(Baha'u'llah, The Arabic
Hidden Words)

The Soul

My soul is the real me, the essence of what I am. Unlike my body which is merely the form through which my soul is expressed in this world, my soul does not need food or drink or sleep. When my body dies and disintegrates, my soul will continue on through the worlds of God. Invisible to the physical senses, it nevertheless can be seen through my actions. It may reveal its knowledge to me in dreams and is an indispensable partner whenever a difficult decision must be made.

The image of my Creator is reflected in the mirror of my soul, or at least it can be. The truer I am to my real self, my spiritual self, the truer I am to God and the more I come to reflect His perfections. Not that I am ever a perfect reflection of Him; that distinction is reserved for the Manifestations of God. I am on an eternal journey through which I can acquire perfections and, I hope, more perfectly polish the mirror of my soul. Moreover, mind is a power of the soul, however many physical conditions may affect its outward manifestation. So it is not enough to perform good acts without thought; I must seek to know good as well as to do good, and to purify my thoughts as well as my actions.

The measure of an action by man is the intent of the action. Therefore one's intentions must be clear in any action one takes. It is possible to have all wrongs forgiven at the time of one's acknowledgement of faith, just as the thief crucified with Jesus was promised being with Him that very day of crucifixion. Judging from this, forgiveness can be granted at confession of faith and belief, but one has to be sure to be steadfast in His love after that. We have had dreams of a strange nature when we do things we could not do in wakefulness, perhaps this is when the soul is travelling. Many of us have had dreams when we walk without using feet and speak without using a mouth. There are dreams we have which actually become fact in wakefulness. When we ponder we speak with a self which is not visible in order to make decisions. Yet there is no physical seat where than inner person resides in the body.

This is the description of the soul the Blessed Beauty gives:

> **LXXXII. Thou hast asked Me concerning the nature of the soul. Know, verily, that the soul is a sign of God, a heavenly gem whose reality the most learned of men hath failed to grasp, and whose mystery no mind, however acute, can ever hope to unravel. It is the first among all created things to declare the excellence of its Creator, the first to recognize His glory, to cleave to His truth, and to bow down in adoration before Him. If it be faithful to God, it will reflect His light, and will, eventually, return unto Him...**

(Baha'u'llah, Gleanings from the Writings of Baha'u'llah, p. 158)

The whole of a person, his soul and body have a connection, which when broken by death, leaves the body to decompose in the earth, while the soul which holds the whole together has to answer for all deeds of life. We, as bodies are processed and reprocessed by the earth. In this view, think of all the earthquakes that have overtaken the earth and buried millions. Think again of how those bodies are processed by animals and plants, and finally think of how much we love eating lamb. If ever one meets a cannibal, it would be wise to treat the matter with some care, remembering who we are in bodies. Our bodies are processed and reprocessed into the earth, in such wise that what we are composed of in food and body has been before as a living thing. Our pride in ourselves as bodies then is futile. We live as bodies in atoms that have known bodies.

As with the General Systems Theory(Syttner), is deemed a truth that nothing is lost, but is retained elsewhere. No one leaves this earth as a perfection, so somehow we leave incomplete, This seems to render the purpose of our creation on a journey to perfection as being incomplete at death. Bahá'ís claim that we proceed to the many worlds of God, ever drawing nearer to the station of being His image in the measure He has given each as our capacity. Leaves are leaves and do not dispute size, why should humans who are a higher intelligence do that?

We are all on the same journey. We are all made in God's image, and He has set before us all the task of developing the potential He has placed within us. Through prayer, meditation, and good works we grow towards Him and increasingly reflect the light of His love. Because we are all on the same journey, no matter how far we progress we cannot claim superiority over others. Indeed, lack of humility itself signals lack of progress. It is is like smudging a well-polished mirror while trying to show off its clarity

The journey is eternal because it reaches for the image of the Eternal. None knows the station of any other. Even a true believer never knows his own station. Only the Deity and His chosen ones would know. We are known in the next world even better than we ourselves know our reality.

"...For this reason it hath been decreed that in this earthly life the full

**measure of the glory of his own station
should remain concealed from the eyes
of such a believer.»** **«If the veil be lifted,
and the full glory of the station of those
who have turned wholly towards God,
and in their love for Him renounced
the world, be made manifest, the entire
creation would be dumbfounded."**

(The Advent of Divine Justice, p. 76)

**Ye are better known to the inmates of
the Kingdom on high than ye are known
to your own selves. Think ye these words
to be vain and empty? Would that ye had
the power to perceive the things your
Lord, the All-Merciful, doth see -- things
that attest the excellence of your rank,
that bear witness to the greatness of
your worth, that proclaim the sublimity
of your station! God grant that your
desires and unmortified passions may
not hinder you from that which hath
been ordained for you.**

(Bahá'u'lláh, Gleanings from the
Writings of Bahá'u'lláh, p. 317)

Reading the Word of God itself is even better than
reading any other book. But each Bahá'í is a teacher and
must show the way in deed and word.

Reaching for Unity

Bahá'u'lláh calls us to unity on a global scale, but it would be naive to expect that such unity can be achieved overnight. We can't simply declare unity and have it be so, as we might cover a cold child with a warm blanket and say, "There, that's better!" The world is destined to become united in the future, but not without a great deal of work. That work must be commence today.

We must first realize that all of the world's most pressing problems are symptoms of its disunity; they cannot be addressed without forging unity. To attempt anything less would be like putting an adhesive strip on a gushing artery. This recognized, we can seek to understand and address the causes of disunity. Such an effort will require sincere and open discussion involving all segments of society. It demands that we put aside all feelings of superiority or inferiority. All must come to the table as equals. The advantaged cannot presume to speak for the disadvantaged, nor should the educated assume they have nothing to learn from those lacking a string of letters after their names. Such discussion cannot occur under threat or with a sense of imposition. The rights of all people and nations must be respected and preserved. While this is a challenging list of requirements, it really boils down to one principle, which Bahá'u'lláh eloquently stated thus:

O SON OF SPIRIT!

The best beloved of all things in My sight is Justice; turn not away therefrom if

thou desirest Me, and neglect it not that I may confide in thee. By its aid thou shalt see with thine own eyes and not through the eyes of others, and shalt know of thine own knowledge and not through the knowledge of thy neighbor. Ponder this in thy heart; how it behooveth thee to be. Verily justice is My gift to thee and the sign of My loving-kindness. Set it then before thine eyes.

(The Hidden Words, Arabic 2)

The earth is but one country, and mankind its citizens.

(Gleanings from the Writings of
Bahá'u'lláh, CXVII, p. 250)

This seems to suggest that God is passive to what man does about unity a notion which is itself a lie for as we know He does instruct us to be cohesive towards one another, for He teaches love, and unity is much a part of that cohesion. There are abounding warnings to mankind if the human fails to heed the law and injunction He gives, especially if one looks at a book by Shoghi Effendi, the Guardian of the Faith, called " The Advent of Divine Justice". It is no mere challenge to say one must on their own read all about the justice the Guardian points to in this book.

The one warning the writer keeps in mind as a daily recital is this:

21. O MOVING FORM OF DUST!

I desire communion with thee, but thou wouldst put no trust in Me. The sword of thy rebellion hath felled the tree of thy hope. At all times I am near unto thee, but thou art ever far from Me. Imperishable glory I have chosen for thee, yet boundless shame thou hast chosen for thyself. While there is yet time, return, and lose not thy chance.

(Bahá'u'lláh, The Persian Hidden Words)

CVIII. We have a fixed time for you, O peoples. If ye fail, at the appointed hour, to turn towards God, He, verily, will lay violent hold on you, and will cause grievous afflictions to assail you from every direction. How severe, indeed, is the chastisement with which your Lord will then chastise you!

(Baha'u'llah, Gleanings from the Writings of Baha'u'llah, p. 214)

The Unity of Religions

A central teaching of the Bahá'í Faith is the unity of

religion. The religions which have been central pillars of human civilization throughout the ages are all considered valid, having been established by Manifestations of God, and thus are equal in rank. They only differ in their outward forms: the languages in which their teachings are recorded; the symbols and metaphors used; their social teachings and laws, which are "prescriptions" for the ages in which they were revealed. The Bahá'í Faith is the newest religion, revealed for all humanity in the present age, leading us toward global unity.

All religions however, are in essence ways of life. They all teach certain core principles, such as the Golden Rule and most of the laws found in the Ten Commandments. Even the names by which God is called, although varying from religion to religion and culture to culture, are variations on a theme. In African cultures alone we find myriad names for the Divine, Unseen Being who provides for all. Often these names utilize symbols from the natural world, but they reflect the perfections of God. I suspect that practices such as idolatry, nature worship, and polytheism derived from such symbolic references to God's attributes. But even in polytheist religions, there is often a singular "Great Being" who is supreme over all things. Even symbols visible in this day or the near past must have had at some stage a relation to the Eternal Being, but have through time found corruption. God could not have left all the world without some form of guidance. We call Him Just, and He is consistent in that. The word we use in religion, and that is "infidel" means one who had a covenant and did not keep his or her share of that covenant with God. Hence at the time of the revelation of any True Manifestation of God, those who oppose are in fact not faithful, and therefore were infidels. This word in Arabic translates into " Kaffir". Those in Africa were regarded as infidels but it soon transpired that they had myriads of names for the Deity, and had not known of recent Manifestations. When most of then heard, they believed. The matter rests there now.

Today we generally recognize that there is but one reality, there can be but one Creator, even though His Names might be legion. Moreover, it must be admitted that each of His Names must describe an attribute that we can only vaguely grasp based on our experience of the creation itself. We are creators, so we can to some degree imagine God as a Creator. But can we truly grasp what it must be to be the Creator of all things, including space and time itself? We have therefore reached a point in our collective history where we have the potential to accept the idea that all religions are on a deep level, one.

Nevertheless it is not always easy to see the connections between differing religions. So I would like to offer a few brief passages for illustration:

> **Sattwan, Raias, and Tamas, so are named**
> **The qualities of Nature, "Soothfastness,"**
> **"Passion," and "Ignorance." These three bind down**
> **The changeless Spirit in the changeful flesh.**
> **Whereof sweet "Soothfastness," by purity**
> **Living unsullied and enlightened, binds**
> **The sinless Soul to happiness and truth;**
> **And Passion, being kin to appetite,**
> **And breeding impulse and propensity,**

Binds the embodied Soul, O Kunti's Son!
By tie of works. But Ignorance, begot
Of Darkness, blinding mortal men, binds down
Their souls to stupor, sloth, and drowsiness.
Yea, Prince of India! Soothfastness binds souls
In pleasant wise to flesh; and Passion binds
By toilsome strain; but Ignorance, which blots
The beams of wisdom, binds the soul to sloth.
Passion and Ignorance, once overcome,
Leave Soothfastness, O Bharata! Where this
With Ignorance are absent, Passion rules;
And Ignorance in hearts not good nor quick.
When at all gateways of the Body shines
The Lamp of Knowledge, then may one see well
Soothfastness settled in that city reigns;
Where longing is, and ardour, and unrest,
Impulse to strive and gain, and avarice,
Those spring from Passion- Prince!- engrained; and where
Darkness and dulness, sloth and stupor are,
Tis Ignorance hath caused them, Kuru Chief!

(Hindu, Bhagavad Gita (Edwin
Arnold tr p. 71))

When Righteousness
Declines, O Bharata! when Wickedness
Is strong, I rise, from age to age, and take

Visible shape, and move a man with men,
Succouring the good, thrusting the evil back,
And setting Virtue on her seat again.
Who knows the truth touching my births on earth
And my divine work, when he quits the flesh
Puts on its load no more, falls no more down
To earthly birth: to Me he comes, dear Prince!

(Hindu, Bhagavad Gita (Edwin Arnold tr p. 2

Many do not know that we are here in this world to live in harmony. Those who know this do not fight against each other.

(Dhammapada, 6 (Wisdom of Buddhism p. 53)

Every action we perform leaves an imprint on our very subtle mind, and each imprint eventually gives rise to its own effect. Our mind is like a field and performing actions is like sowing seeds in that field. Virtuous actions sow seeds of future happiness and non-virtuous actions sow seeds of future suffering

A Meditation handbook, Geshe Gatso (Wisdom of Buddhism., p. 75)

The Guardian's Translations

Many find the Guardian's translations difficult to understand. His use of Elizabethan English—reminiscent of the King James Bible—and the advanced vocabulary he employed do indeed put demands on many people's reading skills. Yet he had the challenge of bringing to the wider world not only the ideas but the hidden meanings and the eloquence of what he called "Bahá'u'lláh's matchless utterance." I feel he did well, creating translations exquisite and dignified without losing the substance of the Word of God.

When I was first asked to translate the *Kitáb-i-Íqán* into Xhosa, I discovered I had much to learn. As the work proceeded and I discussed words with my Persian brothers, I realized my predicament was deeper than I had imagined. Translation requires attention to both meaning and to how that meaning is conveyed. Terms and expressions familiar to the English reader might have no direct equivalent in Xhosa, or might end up sounding strange. For example, iin Arabic the word "create" is "rab". The phrase, "O my God!" would be directly translated as "Ay Rahebi", literally "O my Creator". But in those instances where the phrase is repeated with some alteration, such as "Oh God, my God," the resulting translation, literally "O Creator, my Creator" would sound strange to a speaker of English as this is not always the format we use calling on God.

In other instances, a straightforward translation can result in a convoluted sentence. For example, the sentence Shoghi Effendi translates to English as "Eschew all fellowship with the ungodly," would literally be translated as, "From the evil withhold both hand and heart." No English speaker would say that, nor is it entirely clear what exactly is meant by it. As I learned, the Guardian had addressed such issues over and over during his translation work, and I had to tackle them fresh in taking the *Kitáb-i-Íqán* from English into Xhosa. I have no fluency in either Persian or Arabic, so I only know of such cases by what native speakers of these languages have told me. Nevertheless, my experience taught me that translators must always have their audiences in mind. Even though the Guardian's translations are challenging, I feel they are both merciful and understanding insofar as he accomplished them with such beauty and precision that those who do not know the original languages can, with time and effort, come to fully appreciate the miracle of the Word of God. Certainly it would be best to read it in the original language, but barring the possibility that in the distant future all children will be taught these languages, such translations will be necessary.

One translation which manifestly shows how merciful to readers the Guardian was is that of the Tablet of Ahmad.

In the prayer Book this tablet ends with the words:" **All praise be to God the Lord of all the worlds"**

In the original text there are warnings to humankind that the Guardian felt too strong for even Western ears to understand. So that one sentence of that tablet was left out by him when he translated the Tablet of Ahmad. However that whole Tablet is chanted in entirety in Arabic.

A note on the cover of a Prayer Book belonging to my spiritual mother concerning the Tablet of Ahmad, (Authenticated by Ilona Sala, niece of Emeric Sala, and author of "Tending the Garden").

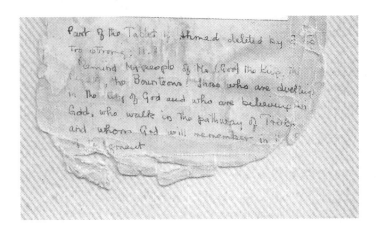

The bottom of the note above, enlarged (Cropped by Robert Mazibuko)

As Guardian's wife indicated, he used to even chant messages to the friends that he wrote to ensure that they sounded just right. (See " The Priceless Pearl" by Hand of the Cause Ruhiyyih Khanum.) So he took pains to translate so that the integrity of the Writings was maintained, and the meaning came through properly without being too edited. As a translator I found that a momentous task, and very trying. I translated from 1969 until I was off the Assembly and even later in 1988 when I was already in the United States. In one book I explained that I used about two Xhosa dictionaries, " Cruden's Concordance" and two English Dictionaries, just to try to come out with a correct meaning of things, some not available in Africa. How much more for a Guardian surrounded on all sides by eager Covenant Breakers in his family, and on both sides of the ocean.. His work on translation is inexplicable under the conditions!

The Guardian had the task of keeping the integrity of the Writings intact even in translations for the sake of posterity, with the view of holding onto the dignity of the Cause at a very difficult time in his life. Viewing even from my distance, I can see how much pain the Guardian must have gone through in those years of wars unrest teaching to the whole world a new faith

Emeric Sala who met the Guardian and produced a paper called:" Shoghi Effendi's Question" remarks in his talk on the question that he "had never seen any man in the faith, who had given so much of himself to the Faith and for the faith and the Guardianship, obliterating all personal concerns and desires". This was as far back as 1939 when the Guardian was himself a youth, and Emeric a new Bahá'í of ten years.(Sala, E).

Knowing this about him and having the experience of translating in Africa, it is a great pain to the writer to hear educated persons in the West complain of the dignity of the English Shoghi Effendi employs in his translations. For he himself knows the difficulties of translating not just words but feelings in the original words used by the Blessed Beauty. None of it is easy!

This may sound very silly but one could look at a translation of English from French Mentioned by George Du Maurier in his book " The Martian: A Novel":

The French would be: "Je Voudrais pouvoir" in which case the translation could be:"I would like to be able." However literally this could also be" I would will to can". If the sentence is reversed to:"Je pourais vouloir", what would stop a child from translating it into" "I would can to will", instead of "I would be able to will"?(Du Maurier, p. 47) The

Guardian avoided this kind of translation. One could look at the large volume of Bahá'í translations in the English language to understand the formidable task the Guardian had, when one takes into account that some of the ideas were not just philosophical but poetic involving much imagery that we could not understand.

Even when he Guardian did not wish his birthday celebrated by the Bahá'ís there is no reason not to celebrate the literature he gave us in his translations. I place her his picture that this be not forgotten:

A final word: A Token of Thanks

My knowledge of the Faith of Bahá'u'lláh developed thanks to the inspiration I received from many fellow Bahá'ís. Foremost were Hand of the Cause Amatu'l-Bahá Rúhíyyih Khánum and my dear spiritual mother, Rosemary Sala. As a token of my gratitude, I would like to share some memories of them.

I first heard Rúhíyyih Khánum, the wife of the beloved Guardian, on a 78-rpm audio recording of her reading the message of the Guardian for the dedication of the Bahá'í House of Worship in Wilmette, Illinois. My spiritual mother Rosemary Sala gave me that recording in 1968 when, to my great sadness, she was about to leave her pioneering post in South Africa. Through Rúhíyyih Khánum›s voice—at once sincere, pleading, and commanding—I caught a glimmer of the reverence the hearts of the believers held for the Word of the Blessed Beauty. So easy was it to remember the words of the prayer she recited that I recall them even now:

O God, Who art the Author of all Manifestations, the Source of all Sources, the Fountain-Head of all Revelations, and the Well-Spring of all Lights! I testify that by Thy Name the heaven of understanding hath been adorned, and the ocean of utterance hath surged, and the dispensations of Thy providence have been promulgated unto the followers of all religions.(Bahá'í Prayers, p. 173)

Lauded and glorified art Thou, O Lord my God! Thou art He Who from everlasting hath been clothed with majesty, with authority and power, and will continue unto everlasting to be arrayed with honor, with strength and glory. The learned, one and all, stand aghast before the signs and tokens of Thy handiwork, while the wise find themselves, without exception, impotent to unravel the mystery of Them Who are the Manifestations of Thy might and power. Every man of insight hath confessed his powerlessness to scale the heights of Thy knowledge, and every man of learning hath acknowledged his failure to fathom the nature of Thine Essence.

Having barred the way that leadeth unto Thee, Thou hast, by virtue of Thine authority and through the potency of

Thy will, called into being Them Who are the Manifestations of Thy Self, and hast entrusted Them with Thy message unto Thy people, and caused Them to become the Day-Springs of Thine inspiration, the Exponents of Thy Revelation, the Treasuries of Thy Knowledge and the Repositories of Thy Faith, that all men may, through Them, turn their faces towards Thee, and may draw nigh unto the kingdom of Thy Revelation and the heaven of Thy grace.

I beseech Thee, therefore, by Thyself and by Them, to send down, from the right hand of the throne of Thy grace, upon all that dwell on earth, that which shall wash them from the stain of their trespasses against Thee, and cause them to become wholly devoted to Thy Self, O Thou in Whose hand is the source of all gifts, that they may all arise to serve Thy Cause, and may detach themselves entirely from all except Thee. Thou art the Almighty, the All-Glorious, the Unrestrained.

(from audio recording by Kelsey's Records)

I finally met Rúhíyyih Khánum in 1985 when I went on pilgrimage with a group from Swaziland. One day while we were in the Holy Land, she gave a short talk and I could not resist the impulse to ask some questions on how the Laws of the Faith related to certain cultural problems plaguing Africa. She advised me to carefully observe the counsel of the National Assembly on such issues. She also suggested that I look up a program called "The Green Light Expedition" and listen carefully to the suggestions she made there. I did so, and still apply it today.

Later the pilgrims were invited to "high tea" at her home. She asked me to perform an African dance. I admitted that I knew very little about African dances; at my college we were more likely to jitterbug! So instead, she then asked me for some other form of "South African performance". I told a short story in clicks. When I explained the meaning of the tale in English, which did not seem like much even to myself, she pointed out that outside of the clicks the story said very little, and of course she was right.

I was impressed when she said that on her tombstone she wished for only two words: "I tried". I visited her resting place in Haifa in 2015 to see those words for myself.

Resting place of the Hand of the Cause 'Amatu'l-Bahá Ruḥíyyíh Khanum(Picture taken in 2015 by author during pilgrimage)

And thus to Rosemary. Rosemary Sala's life, along with that of her husband Emeric, is recounted in *Tending the Garden* by Ilona Weinstein-Sala. I have also mentioned her in all of the other books that I have written. As you can see from her photo, she had a very direct gaze. Her gaze mirrored her manner. She was always direct with me and if she sensed something was wrong with me, physically or spiritually, she sometimes wouldn't even allow me to leave her apartment until I had told her about it.

She was both caring and tough, helping me through my life as a young teenager, but insisting that I get out into the world and support myself once I was out of high school. She found me my first job, setting me on the road to becoming a hospital clerk. When I wanted to go to college, she insisted

I seek a loan from the university and that I be ready to pay it back. She would not give me one penny except to provide me with traveling bags and clothing. Yet she supplied the birthday cake for my twenty-first birthday.

When I returned home for vacation, Rosemary urged me to find work so I could support myself. At that time—the early sixties—many sought "imperial moneys"—government support—for their education. But Rosemary regarded self-support as vital, even when a Bahá'í travelled to teach the Faith, as I eventually did. I was asked by the National Assembly of Southern Africa to spend my school vacation traveling to the Transkei, to which I had never been, to help elect delegates to the National Bahá'í Convention. Rosemary observed that I would need a raincoat for the rainy summers of that land, and mentioned that she had seen some inexpensive ones at the OK Bazaars in the city. She wanted me to buy one, and insisted that I put up a certain sum for its purchase. I gave her the money, she bought the coat for me. I wore that coat for years, but more importantly, because I paid my own way others could see that I wasn't a Bahá'í because I received material benefits from it.

Rosemary often quoted a line from Tennyson's Ulysses: "I am part of all that I have met." (*Ulysses*, line 18.) In letters she wrote to me from Mexico, she frequently said she oft heard the voices and saw all those faces she had left in Africa. Nor was she forgotten by any of us. In teaching the Faith, she often recited a passage from Bahá'u'lláh's Writings, one that she lived as well as spoke. I can think of no better way to close that by sharing it with you:

Be generous in prosperity, and thankful in adversity. Be worthy of the

trust of thy neighbor, and look upon him with a bright and friendly face. Be a treasure to the poor, an admonisher to the rich, an answerer to the cry of the needy, a preserver of the sanctity of thy pledge. Be fair in thy judgment, and guarded in thy speech. Be unjust to no man, and show all meekness to all men. Be as a lamp unto them that walk in darkness, a joy to the sorrowful, a sea for the thirsty, a haven for the distressed, an upholder and defender of the victim of oppression. Let integrity and uprightness distinguish all thine acts. Be a home for the stranger, a balm to the suffering, a tower of strength for the fugitive. Be eyes to the blind, and a guiding light unto the feet of the erring. Be an ornament to the countenance of truth, a crown to the brow of fidelity, a pillar of the temple of righteousness, a breath of life to the body of mankind, an ensign of the hosts of justice, a luminary above the horizon of virtue, a dew to the soil of the human heart, an ark on the ocean of knowledge, a sun in the heaven of bounty, a gem on the diadem of wisdom, a shining light in the firmament of thy generation, a fruit upon the tree of humility...

(Epistle to the Son of the Wolf, p. 93)

Rosemary Sala, my spiritual parent.(Picture gift from Ilona Sala niece of Rosemary Sala and author of "Tending the Garden")

Epilogue

When a children first enter school, they learn the alphabet. Soon they discover how letters form words and begin to read and write. Over time, they adds words to her vocabulary and delve deeper into grammar and style. If they persist, over time they acquire sufficient writing skill to compose complex works like term papers and books.

This is progressive development. It characterizes all aspects of life. We are not born running marathons. First we learn to crawl, then to stand, then to walk and run. Each lesson builds on the next, fulfilling what went before. Even though the lessons of the past may fade in memory, they are never truly forgotten, for without them we would not be where we are. This is why I have never forgotten how I came to be a Bahá'í and to love my religion. I would not be what I am today had those events not taken place.

At present there is much hurt in the world and many swear vengeance. The world has to learn to move forward, and build on the past. It is not wise to relive the past every day of one's life, but far easier to face the problems of the day, for the past cannot be altered but the future can. We have to forgive one another, without having to forget the lesson of experience. In most cases logic will say one thing, while wisdom advises against. We all have a past and have learned through that past. How we use the past to determine our future safe behavior, becomes critical. Experience is a great director and we should not allow our old to leave without at least leaving some of it behind so that our children never have to start from scratch about everything we have already learned.

In our age lies the value for the future. What we know cannot and must not be treated as garbage by youth, for it stands as a witness to what occurs when certain things are not observed in any society. It is true that a statement of blanket peace, does not help. But it is also true that bringing things to the table and allowing consultation can go a long way towards peace. No one wants to be forced into a situation, for once one is forced into it,one does not have to take any responsibility for results. One can always say:"I was not consulted". We are all human and need that respect of being asked for what we are going to serve in. Cromwell is reported in a movie as having said about the poor" Being poor and simple people, they would like to be asked for what is theirs", a true statement. Every man is a knight in his castle. That has to be respected. To decide for one about things one knows best about is not wisdom at all. To a certain measure, that is one reason the world is the way it is today. Too many decide for too many, too many times, and leave them out of that decision except to obey. That is not human respect, but human degradation. That has to come to an and end soon.

'Abdu'l-Baha, was the Center of the Covenant of His

Father, but all He said of Himself, bearing in mind that "abd" means a servant, was the following:

> **"My name is 'Abdu'l-Bahá. My qualification is 'Abdu'l-Bahá. My reality is 'Abdu'l-Bahá. My praise is 'Abdu'l-Bahá. Thralldom to the Blessed Perfection[1] is my glorious and refulgent diadem, and servitude to all the human race my perpetual religion... No name, no title, no mention, no commendation have I, nor will ever have, except 'Abdu'l-Bahá. This is my longing. This is my greatest yearning. This is my eternal life. This is my everlasting glory.**
>
> ('Abdu'l-Bahá, quoted in Adib Taherzadeh, p. 26)

The following is from Bahá'u'lláh Himself:

> **The source of courage and power is the promotion of the Word of God, and steadfastness in His Love.**
>
> (*Tablets of Bahá'u'lláh*, p. 156)

> **This is the Day whereon the Ocean of God's mercy hath been manifested unto men, the Day in which the Day**

Star of His loving-kindness hath shed its radiance upon them, the Day in which the clouds of His bountiful favor have overshadowed the whole of mankind. Now is the time to cheer and refresh the down-cast through the invigorating breeze of love and fellowship, and the living waters of friendliness and charity

(Gleanings from the Writings of Bahá'u'lláh, p. 6)

In his later years, one of my Bahá'í mentors, Cassiem Davids, taught me to recite the following prayer. It was his favorite in the Arabic language and holds much meaning for me, personally. I can think of no better way to close.

Create in me a pure heart, O my God, and renew a tranquil conscience within me, O my Hope! Through the spirit of power confirm Thou me in Thy Cause, O my Best-Beloved, and by the light of Thy glory reveal unto me Thy path, O Thou the Goal of my desire! Through the power of Thy transcendent might lift me up unto the heaven of Thy holiness, O Source of my being, and by the breezes of Thine eternity gladden me, O Thou Who art my God! Let Thine everlasting melodies breathe tranquility on me, O my Companion, and let the riches of Thine ancient countenance deliver me

from all except Thee, O my Master, and let the tidings of the revelation of Thine incorruptible Essence bring me joy, O Thou Who art the most manifest of the manifest and the most hidden of the hidden!"

(Bahá'u'lláh, *Bahá'í Prayers*, p. 142)

Glossary

Abu Refers to "father"

Asma Names

Athim A Sinner

Bábí Faith A Faith that preceded that of Bahá'u'lláh in Iran

Baynul Both

Bayan Discourse

Firdous Paradise

Hu Pronoun indicating third person

Hud A Manifestation mentioned in the Qur'an and in the Kitáb-i-Iqán

Ibn Refers to Son

Iqan Certitude

Ism Name

Kaaba A shrine of Islam in Saudi rabia, Mecca, which is circled by pilgrims as the center of their faith or Qiblih or Point of Adoration.

Kabah. A version of "Kaaba" in English alphabet

Kalimat Words

Karim Honorable

Kitab Book

Mulla and Islamic priest

Mujthid A doctor of Islamic law

Qaim The Promised One of Islam Who to Baha'is is the coming of he Báb

Qiblih A direction to which believers turn in offering some certain prayers. To Muslims for example that is Mecca and to Baha'is it is Bahji in Israel where the remains of their Manifestation lie interred.

Qayyum The Eternal One

Quddus Holy One

Qur'an Recital

Saladdhin The name given to Sala –id-din-Jusuf Ibni Ayubi. A general in the Islamic army during the Crusades

Salih A Manifestation mentioned in the Bible, in the Qur'an and the Kitáb-i-Iqán

Tahirih The Pure One. A name given to the first woman to believe in the Báb and therefore one of the Letters of the Living, the first eighteen to believe in Him. Her real name was Umm Salima.

Ulama A person of high rank in the hierarchy of the Islamic Faith

References

'Abdu'l-Bahá. *Memorials of the Faithful*. Wilmette, IL. Bahá'í Publishing Trust.

'Abd'ul-Bahá. *Selections from the Writings of 'Abdu'l-Bahá*. Haifa, Israel. Bahá'í World Center.

Adin Taherzadeh. *Revelation of Bahá'ulláh vol. II*. Oxford, UK. George Ronald.

Arnold, E.(1993) *Bhagavad Gita. A Translation*. New York, NY. Dover Publications Inc.

Bahá'u'lláh. *The Hidden Words of Baha'u'llah*. Wilmette, IL. Bahá'í Publishing Trust.

Bahá'u'lláh. *Kitab-i-Aqdás*. Wilmette, IL. Bahá'í Publishing Trust

Bhá'u'lláh.*Kitáb-i-Iqán*. Wilmette, IL. Bahá'í Publishing Trust..

Bahá'u'lláh *The Seven Valleys and the Four Valleys*. Wilmette, IL. Bahá'í Publishing Trust.

Bahá'u'lláh. *Tablets of Bahá'u'lláh*. Haifa, Israel. Bahá'í World

Publishing Trust. *Bahá'í Prayers*. Wilmette. IL. Bahá'í Publishing Trust.

Bahá'u'lláh Epistle to the Son of the Wolf. Wilmette, IL. Bahá'í Publishing Trust.

Shoghi Effendi. Faith, *Gleanings from the Writings of Baha'ullah*.Wilmette, Il. Bahá'í Publishing Trust.

Du Maurier, G..The *Marian: A Novel*. Bibliolife.

Dunbar, H. Comments after a summer school. Made after service at the Universal House of Justice. Durant, W. & A.(1961) The Age of Reason Begins. New York, NY. Simon and Schuster

Encyclopedia Britannica *Biela's Comet*

Picture retrieved 04/07/2017 from

h t t p s : / / i m a g e s . s e a r c h . y a h o o . c o m / s e a r c h / i m a g e s ? p = b e i l a % 2 7 s + c o m e t & f r = y f p - t & i m g u r l = h t t p % 3 A % 2 F % 2 F t h u n d e r b o l t s . info%2Ftpod%2F2006%2Fimage06%2F060207biela. jpg#id=1&iurl=http%3A%2F%2Fthunderbolts. info%2Ftpod%2F2006%2Fimage06%2F060207biela. jpg&action=click

WRITTEN BY:

THe EDITORS OF ENCYCLOPEDIA BRITANNICA

LAST UPDATED:

6-23-2014

Article

Retrieved April 7, 2017 from:

See Arhttps://www.britannica.com/topic/Bielas-Cometticle History

Holy Bible. King James version. Michigan, USA. Zondevan.

Hornby, H.(1983) *Lights of Guidance*. Delhi. India. Bahá'í Publishing Trust.

Hymnary.org. *The song of minutes*.

Retrieved on 05/27/2017 from

http://hymnary.org/text/we_are_but_minutes_little_things

Jung, C. G.(1963) *Memories Dreams, Reflections*. New York, NY. Vintage Books.

Marlowe, C. (1984) *Doctor Faustus*. UK. Longman Group UK Ltd.

Nakhjavani, A Comments after a talk in the United States/ Canada.

Outlet Book Company(1982) *Works of Charles Dickens*. New York, NY. Chatam River Press..

Perry, M. *Western Civilization*. Boston. USA. Houghton Mifflin Company.

Publishing Trust(1992). *Bahá'í Prayers*. Wilmette, IL. Bahá'í Publishing Trust

Sala. E. *Shoghi Effendi's Question, a paper*.(from cassette and CD recording)

Shoghi Effendi. *Advent of Divine Justice*. Wilmette, IL. Bahá'í Publishing Trust.

Shoghi Effendi. *The Dawn Breakers.. A translation from Nabil's Narrative by Nabil of Zarand*. Wilmette, IL. Bahá'í Publishing Trust.

Shoghi Effendi., *Gleanings from the Writings of Baha'ullah*. Wilmette, Il. Bahá'í Publishing Trust. Trust.

Shoghi Effendi.*The Promised Day is Come*. Wilmette, IL. Bahá'í Publishing Trust.

Skyttner, L.(2007) *General Systems Theory*. New Jersey, USA. World
Scientific.

Tennyson, Lord. *The beggar Maid*.
　　Retrieved on 05/27/2017 from
　　https://genius.com/Alfred-lord-tennyson-the-beggar-maid-annotated

Thompson, M(2000). *The Wisdom of Buddhism*. Oxford, UK. One World..

Tyfeld., T, Nicol. K.R.(1960) *The Living Tradition*. Cape Town, South Africa, Maskew Miller Ltd.

Van Dooren Stern, P.(1977) *Portable Shakespeare*. New York, NY. Penguin Group

Printed in the United States
By Bookmasters